The NOWHERE *Road*

Elmstead Publications
Milestone Lane
Wicklewood
Norfolk
NR18 9QL
www.norfolkbooks.com

© Bruce Robinson

Elmstead Publications
Milestone Lane
Wicklewood
Norfolk NR18 9QL
www.norfolkbooks.com

ISBN 0 9523379 32

British Library Cataloguing in Publication Data. A catalogue
record for this book is available from the British Library

Text input and book design by the author using a DTP system
with PageMaker 6.5. Main text font: Times Roman

Printed by Geo Reeve Ltd, Wymondham, Norfolk

Pictures and diagrams by the author unless stated otherwise

Front cover photograph: The Peddars Way near Shakers Furze,
Thompson, in Breckland

Well sometimes I got the notion
That I've got to hit the road,
So I hit the oldest road in the land . . .
(Tony Maude, poet, songwriter, 1994)

Foreword

BETWEEN these covers Bruce has mapped out the complete history (as he sees it, at present) of the Peddars Way.
When you walk the Peddars Way you tread history, as the Dutch *Op Pad* reporter found: "In the dark pubs of Norfolk there are whispers that all is not well on the Peddars Way. Terrible things have happened on the old Roman road, so it will be haunted for eternity. Just keep walking. Pretend not to see the phantom-like riders. Do not look up when horses gallop through your tent, chariots thunder past you, and all around you hear the groans of slain Saxons. In Norfolk, people prefer to stay well clear of the Peddars Way. If you are stubborn and walk there anyway, you will find there is a beautiful road, a bit lonely and a bit spooky. Whatever you do, don't go on your own." (*Translated from Op Pad, the Dutch walking magazine, 1995*).

Peddars Way, the Roman road, is old. During a period when we have learned to destroy our landscape at will, warp the natural process of evolution by modifying genes, and spend most of our lives divorced from the reality of the land, this road has marched through our landscape with uncanny certainty. On its journey through time, the Way has witnessed two millennia of British landscape history, from flint knapping to Iron Age village, medieval buildings and pilgrims, enclosures to post-war agricultural intensification. And after many decades of neglect the route, in the past 20 years, has undergone a rebirth. In 2002 the Peddars Way National Trail reaches its 15th birthday, and during those 15 years it will have felt the weight of over one million walkers and 100,000 cyclists and horse riders.

The Way was born out of an incident of national, if not international, significance. Two thousand years on it is again on the same stage, as a national route used by the British Tourist Authority to promote walking in Britain to the world.

A landscape comes to life when one is aware of the past. Explore this book, follow in the footsteps of our ancestors, and begin to understand how the past has affected the future. - **Tom Lidstone-Scott**

By the same author

A History of Long Sutton (South Lincolnshire) (with FW Robinson) Produced privately 1965
The Peddars Way The Weathercock Press 1978
A Skylark Descending (novel) Robert Hale 1978
History of Long Sutton & District (with FW Robinson) Long Sutton Civic Trust 1981 Reprinted 1995
Norfolk Origins: 1 Hunters to First Farmers (with Andrew Lawson) Acorn Editions 1981
Norfolk Origins: 2 Roads & Tracks (with Edwin Rose) Poppyland Publishing 1983
The Peddars Way & Norfolk Coast Path Countryside Commission 1986
Norfolk Origins: 3 Celtic Fire & Roman Rule (with Tony Gregory) Poppyland Publishing 1987
Peddars Way & Norfolk Coast Path Aurum Press 1992 Reprinted 1996

As a self-publisher:

Norfolk Fragments Elmstead Publications 1994
A Glimpse of Distant Hills (novel) Elmstead Publications 1995
Chasing the Shadows: Norfolk Mysteries Revisited Elmstead Publications 1996 Reprinted 2000
Passing Seasons: A watching brief on 50 years of football Elmstead Publications 1997
The Norfolk Walker's Book Elmstead Publications 1998
Hudson's Drove (novel) Elmstead Publications 2000

Does the road wind up-hill all the way?
Yes, to the very end.
Will the day's journey take the whole long day?
From morn to night, my friend.
(Christina Rossetti, 'Up-hill,' 1858)

Introduction

THIS is a book about Norfolk's portion of the Peddars Way, which has been an interest of mine for almost thirty years. It follows that the writing of it owes more to a slow accumulation of books, cuttings, ideas, photos, experiences, facts and fictions than to bouts of academic research. However, many people have also helped me, including walking colleagues, interested bystanders and numerous authors, most of whom are listed in Reading & References. I have also been helped, recently and in the past, by Edwin Rose, Robin Brown, the late Tony Gregory, and by David Gurney, Principal Landscape Archaeologist (Norfolk). Their courses and advice (which in one memorable case was, 'Now, tear it up and start again') has, I hope, steered me away from at least a few flights of fancy. I am greatly indebted, too, to Tim Lidstone-Scott (National Trail Manager, Peddars Way & Norfolk Coast Path), to the National Trail Office (6 Station Road, Wells next the Sea, Norfolk, NR23 1AE), and to Norfolk County Council. Tim supplied a great deal of back-up when I was writing the second re-issue of the Peddars Way & Norfolk Coast Path National Trail guidebook, and he has contributed advice and a very kind Foreword to this book. My thanks also go to: Dr Julie Gardiner of The Prehistoric Society for permission to use photographs from Proceedings of the Prehistoric Society of East Anglia, vol 2 part 1, 1914/15; Gerry Moore of GM Designs, for permission to use pen and ink drawings by the cycling artist Frank Patterson; Jan Allen (Norfolk Museums and Archaeology Service, at Gressenhall) for her help in the matter of aerial photographs; the Museums Service for permission to use photographs; Naomi Tummons, Methuen Publishing, for permission to quote from HV Morton's book In Search of England; and to George R Reeve Ltd, my splendid Wymondham printers who also allowed me to quote from RD Clover's book Dim Corridors. The text is ordered as logically as I can make it, which means that subjects follow each other in more or less chronological order. All the errors, of course, are mine. - **Bruce Robinson**

To everyone who has ever walked the Way,
and to anyone who is thinking of doing so

Chapter One

The ghost under the grass

WE ARE a very long way in terms of time and outlook from the sun and shadow inter-war period when HV Morton wrote his In Search of England, published in 1927. Consequently, I do not know the circumstances or inspiration of it, or his particular frame of mind at the time, but I like to think the words for the Peddars Way section came to him on a sultry afternoon when, wearied by long hours of tramping and mellowed by a pint of Norfolk mild and bitter, he sank on to a grass verge beside the Way in the shade of a tree, and instead of sleeping began to scribble.

'I am writing this beside the old road. Where I sit I can see the ghost of it under the grass, broad and embanked, slipping into the distance over the fields. Here it is drenched in deep gloom. The thick trees which hedge it arch themselves above it, and in the hush of this still afternoon I fancy that the leaves have just stopped whispering together of the things that once went by along the Peddars Way.'

Where was he? Knettishall, Thorpe Farm? Thompson, perhaps. Or Harpley. It could have been anywhere. Certainly his was a mind in reflective mode, for this misty dimension is also apparent in his feelings for the road's past and for the passing parade of time and history. Centuries and soldiers, travellers and peasants and pilgrims. Then, suddenly, it seems he also sensed the parade was over and that the grass was growing again.

'The silence of death lives over the Peddars Way . . . A man can walk many a mile in solitude over this ghost of a mighty road . . .'

In 1948, some 20 years later and shortly after the end of a second ghastly world war, RD Clover wrote in Dim Corridors in much the same vein and of a similar sort of expressive silence. He said the Peddars Way, one of England's lost roads, had passed into disuse hundreds of years earlier because the place it was laid down to reach had disappeared and there was nowhere for it to go.

'Trees took root along its grassy verges, grew and flourished, died and fell. Countless generations of rabbits burrowed in the sandy banks alongside and kicked out the sand with their strong hind legs. The bracken and the bramble marched alongside and sometimes the plough passed over it. Yet Peddars Way endures, and today one may walk for miles along this great green Way with only solitude for a companion - a solitude heavy with the aura of forgotten years.'

In one sense the Way has always been heavy with solitude because by and large it ignores and avoids human habitation, so fixedly is its mind set on reaching the coast. And yet this is the road which is said to have nowhere to go. The nowhere road. But make no mistake, it is no dead road. See it in spring and early June when it is alive with blossom and greenery, poppies and dog roses, bracken, pines and hedgerows, partridges, skylarks and butterflies. However, it is difficult to know exactly when the Way did begin to slumber its way into unpopularity and decline, if decline is the right word; perhaps it was after the Reformation when, according to Leonard Whatmore, pious pilgrims bound for Walsingham presumably no longer wended their way along portions of it. This may also have been the time when the old road began to turn its back on its original, long-distance role to become, instead, a local backwater and facility. Whatever the truth, Morton's echoes of the past and Clover's silences and forgotten years remain as quiet tributes to this most amiable of ancient tracks. You can sense the atmosphere still, even today, something more than mere romance or whimsy and certainly more than simple nostalgia. Sometimes it is as if the road itself is speaking, as though voices from the past are still clamouring to be heard.

The irony is that the Peddars Way always was a working road - for marching and riding, for travelling and transporting, for business and trading - and, if you add agriculture, tourism and relaxation, it still is. So what is its appeal? The fact that it is Norfolk's best known and best preserved Roman road. That helps. So does its directness and its unprepossessing solitude, for it is still possible, in places, to walk for an hour or two without seeing another living soul save perhaps a glimpse of a solitary worker in the far corner of a lonely field. All this helps, too. But I think subtlety has much to do with it.

Some roads and many National Trails boast cliffs to scramble, bogs to traverse, rocks to climb and inclines to bring you puffing to the edge of exhaustion. In other words, they are formidable physical tests. The Peddars Way has none of these and is thus usually classified as an 'easy' or 'moderate' walk - which can also be interpreted as boring. But the Way's grandeur is a beauty of a different scale, embracing a slow, gentle shift from Suffolk heath to Norfolk Breck, from forestry to farming, and from 'high' Norfolk landscape to sea level salt marsh. And the road's history? Even that is subtle and obscure, too. Yet the road remains a nice, bracing walk. Refreshing white wine rather than rough and boisterous red.

But see how the perception has shifted. Now it is no longer a matter of transport and communication, marching feet and rumbling carts. Now it is strolling and cycling, peace and quiet, an occasional farm tractor, wildlife, huge skies and the smell of good Norfolk air blowing from the coast. The Peddars Way, the nowhere road, has re-invented itself, banishing some of the ghosts, and I for one am delighted. What I want to do in this book is to describe the Way as it is today, nearly 2000 years after it was built, and to try to look at who might have built it, and equally importantly, when and why. It is the latter questions which in some ways are the most difficult to deal with, for at the moment there are no completely satisfying answers.

However, to attempt all this it is necessary, first, to know something about the local landscape before the Romans came, and second, something about the people who lived there.

The lie of the land

We are fortunate in Norfolk that the landscape is consist- ently varied and variable. In some areas the patterns seem to change from one mile to the next. Beach, forest, cliff, breck, broad, arable upland, reed-bed, fen, boulder clay, saltmarsh, and so on. Even the soil types hint at an ava- lanche of variation. The sub-regions are known as Breckland (the Thetford and Swaffham areas), West Norfolk lowland (east of King's Lynn), Wensum sand (north and west of Norwich), Broadland and Flegg (the Broads area), black fen (inland of King's Lynn), marshland (west of Lynn), boulder clay plateau (Central Norfolk), rich loam (North East Norfolk), Good Sands (high ground of the north-west), Cromer ridge (Holt and Cromer area), and the chalk scarp (roughly, Castle Acre to Holme).

But when all is said and done this is only one chapter of the story. In rudimentary terms Norfolk consists of a series of sedimentary deposits laid down in sometimes confused sequences. Later, the sequences became tilted so that while some of the earliest layers are now exposed at the surface in the north-west Hunstanton area, most of them are buried deep in the east. One example is that of the chalk deposit, which in the north-west outcrops near the surface but in the east is buried below Great Yarmouth at a depth of more than 180 metres. The tilting gives the county a pronounced nautical list.

A further major influence was the crushing, pushing and gouging effects, in the dim and distant past, of successive sequences of ice sheets and melt waters. For example, during the last 800,000 years or so there have been five warm periods (interglacials), labelled Pastonian, Cromerian, Hoxnian, Ipswichian and Flandrian, which we are continuing to enjoy today; and four spells of glaciation (Beestonian, Anglian, Wolstonian and, the most recent, Devensian). During the Anglian and Wolstonian stages the region that is now Norfolk was completely covered by massive ice sheets. It has even been calculated that the last icy spell, the Devensian, which merely touched the tip of North West Norfolk, took about 10,000 years to melt back to the present glacier limits. This was also the time, of course, when some of Norfolk's lakes were formed.

It was the shattering, obliterating Anglian glaciation which had such a profound effect on Norfolk's shape, soil and drainage patterns, and by implication and in consequence, on early colonisation and agriculture.

Inevitably, there were other forces at play, too. Below the marks of the Anglian glacial period yet more layers of gravels and river deposits indicate the former courses of a long-lost water drainage system, now called the Bytham river, which once flowed north-east from the Midlands, turned east near Leicester and crossed into what is now the Fens, and then swung south close to present-day King's Lynn to join the ancestral Thames at or near Bury St

Right: early beginnings at Roudham Heath

Edmunds. In those days it eventually departed from our area roughly in the vicinity of present-day Cromer and West Runton.

This huge and ancient waterway system was in turn destroyed by subsequent glaciations, but traces of the Bytham river's gravels still survive, like a faint memory of the past. Later, the watercourse which ultimately became the Thames migrated south, while the by now much modified Bytham continued to flow across North East Norfolk, leaving the present coastline somewhere between Lowestoft and Southwold. However, the Bytham drainage system does seem to have provided a framework for the area's landscape at the time of the first known human activity in Norfolk, possibly 500,000 years ago. The earliest East Anglians evidently lived and worked beside its banks. Thus it can be seen that this continual glacial process of advance, melt and retreat, allied to big rises in temperature during the interglacials, so scraped, smoothed and rippled the landscape that they finally produced most of the contours we see today.

But nothing ever stays still. Norfolk, over the centuries, has lost a great deal of land to the sea, particularly in the north and north-west; but, and other than at times of flooding, the sea is also withdrawing at various places once again. You can see the effects of this at Blakeney, for example. And yet, driven by rising sea levels, it is advancing at other places along the east coast, nibbling at defences, relishing the thought of breaking inland again. Thus the shape of Norfolk today is merely a snapshot of a single fleeting moment in time. It was certainly not the same yesterday and it will quite definitely not be the same tomorrow.

It needs to be remembered, too, that until about 6400BC Britain was still joined to the Continent by a now-submerged environment which once stretched from North Yorkshire and round Dogger Bank to join the western shore of Jutland. In those days the North Sea Basin, or The Ancient Land, is thought to have been a vast wet landscape of silver birch forest (fragments of ancient woodland material, called moorlog, can still be picked up on the beach in the Titchwell area), scrub, swamp and freshwater pools, through which animals, and, almost certainly humans, were able to tread their careful way. When sea levels finally began to rise about 9,000 years ago the basin succumbed to inundation and Britain subsequently became an island.

It is also worth mentioning that today most of Norfolk's rivers, aside from the Great Ouse, are generally of relatively modest width, and drift seawards at a fairly leisurely pace. Clearly, early settlers tended to prefer the river valleys, for at times when populations were low then the higher lands (the interfluves) could be used, perhaps seasonally, for woodland and pasture. Also, the requirements of settlement and farm meant they usually needed to be less than a mile from rivers or meres. There was the added bonus that rivers, valleys and interfluves offered some defensive possibilities.

One of the last areas to be developed for farming may have been the watershed which, as defined by Tom Williamson, ran in an arc north to south across Norfolk between the rivers Yare, Wensum, Waveney, Tas and Tud, and others, which drain towards the former estuary near Yarmouth; the Nar, Thet and Wissey, which drain west to the Wash; and the Glaven, Burn and Stiffkey, which discharge into the North Sea. The watershed may have been a relatively remote area of reduced contact, a social and political buffer zone where woodland was still to be found even at the time of Domesday.

The Roman Peddars Way enters Norfolk through Breckland and in general hugs the chalk ridge of North West Norfolk's Good Sands region, staying tentatively on the rising slopes of the ridge. The Icknield Way seems to dog its footsteps every inch of the way, though it was marginally lower on the escarpment, slightly to the west and a shade closer to the Wash.

It is interesting that an elementary profile of Norfolk's stretch of the Way, calculated by myself from Ordnance Survey 1:25,000 maps and read from the nearest contour every 400 yards or so, shows remarkably little variation because of Norfolk's relatively placid - as opposed to dramatic - terrain. Beginning at about 75ft above sea level near Knettishall (which is actually in Suffolk, but by only a few hundred yards) and ending at about 25ft as it approaches Holme and the coast, the Way climbs towards 300ft on only three occasions, all of those either at or close to Shepherd's Bush, north of Castle Acre. Thus the general variation of the Norfolk route, from start to finish, is never much more than 275ft, which indicates a fairly benign progression with only a handful of generally modest gradients.

Of even more significance, I feel, is the roughly NW-SE direction of the Way. In Norfolk, and in general terms, this has always been the more difficult route for lines of communication because of the pattern of drainage, water courses and rivers. In this sense the purposeful onward march of the Way seems to go against the natural grain of the landscape reinforcing a feeling that, because this was

The shadows of autumn are etched across the Peddars Way at the start of the National Trail at Knettishall Heath, Suffolk

one of the more complicated directions to take, it was constructed for a very specific purpose.

As already mentioned, however, a precedent had already been set in a much earlier age by the gradual emergence of the Icknield Way.

An early way forward

A cloud of mystery has always hovered over the seemingly impenetrable origins of the Icknield Way, to begin with because no-one was quite sure of its precise route, if there ever was a precise route. Truth to tell, no-one is entirely sure of its route even now, but one or two factors, other than the date of its arrival on the local landscape, have been if not precisely clarified then at least refined. Whether or not it did have an influence on the Peddars Way, or at least on those members of Romano-British society fortunate enough to be able to buy or build agricultural estates and who chose North West Norfolk as their rural retreat (See: The country life) is another matter open to discussion. The problem is that there is very little preciseness at all about the Icknield Way. For example, when did the route first emerge? It is generally held that even if there were enough people in East Anglia's pre-Devensian world, and

Right: crossing the Little Ouse, the county border

even if they were sufficiently regular in their habits and activities to actually form tracks, none of these very early routes would have survived the long, devastating phases of glaciation and centuries of melt. In effect, it is thought the surface of the land would have been scraped clean of the hand (or footfall) of humankind. It follows, therefore, that those routes of antiquity which do survive are unlikely to be more than 10,000 years old. Which is very old, anyway. Where did the Icknield Way it go? Again, there is great uncertainty, but a route of this sort seems to have run along the Chilterns, skirted Fenland and entered present-day Norfolk at Thetford, from whence at least one branch seems to have forded the Little Ouse river at Red Castle and continued towards the coast, or more particularly, Ringstead. This locality has always been perceived as different, in some unknown way, and very important. But even if it did lead towards or even on to the North Sea basin, as seems at least possible, there is no precise evidence for it. Indeed, there is no trace of the route at all beyond Ringstead. If there was a dividing junction of the Icknield at Thetford, then the other branch might have crossed the river near Nuns Bridges and headed in the Norwich direction.

In North West Norfolk, at least during the early Roman period, the route may have resembled an ill-defined network of tracks or droveways running along the marginally higher ground slightly above and to the east of the spring line. Other evidence suggests that between Grimston and Gayton Thorpe it boasted a seasonal diversion, with a drier strand presumably favoured in winter, and a shorter summer route closer to the springs.

How important the Icknield Way was, or whether there were other similar or even more important routes, is beyond the scope of this book. But it seems to have been in use during the Neolithic period, when it might have been a trading artery and could have been an important ingredient in the distribution of flint and other goods.

Again, it is equally possible its origins are to be found in early animal migration routes, when hunting groups in seasonal camps kept watch from the higher ground on herds moving on the North Sea basin.

What does seem clear is that the Icknield Way, particularly before its existence was clarified during the Roman period, was not a single route but a swathe of tracks heading in roughly the same direction. So, was there a pre-Roman 'Peddars Way' route which coincided with one of these tangled strands, as some writers in the past have claimed? Was a portion of the present Peddars Way originally a strand of the Icknield Way? North of Castle Acre, particularly, it certainly looks possible. The two routes seem to hustle along on a very similar line, while in the extreme north-west they run in remarkably close proximity. But this is speculation. There is no evidence either way.

Another glance at the scenery

The dawn of the age of iron (in Norfolk, circa 700-650BC) to the end of the Roman occupation of Britain (circa AD410) spanned a period of perhaps 1100 years. In terms of time this is roughly equivalent to the separation of the Millenium Dome from the death of King Alfred. It goes without saying that in landscape terms, as in everything else, a great deal changed. Many times. And so it was with Norfolk's landscape during the Iron Age and Roman periods.

General fluctuations in sea and land levels, in conjunction with purely local variations, make particular coastlines very difficult to reconstruct. The Late Roman shore forts give one indication of the complexity of the problem. Burgh Castle shore fort is now a sufficient distance inland to indicate there were rises in sea levels during the Roman period of between one and four metres, depending on the precise location. Also, during the early Roman period there

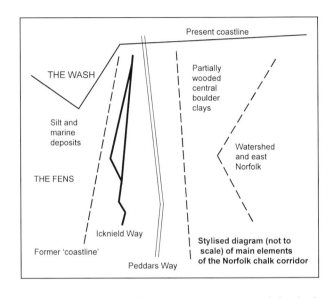

was a huge expansion of the marine deposit areas inland of the present-day Wash, making the Fens a much more significant presence on the map than they are today, and reinforcing the feeling of an older Norfolk 'coastline' running roughly south from present-day King's Lynn perhaps as far as Downham Market. To the west of this 'coastline' the Fens were largely a chain of lagoons and

Above: Parish boundary marker beside the Way near Rushford

Left: The ghost under the grass. Faint signs of an agger mark the progress of the Peddars Way at Thorpe Woodlands as the road approaches the River Thet 'islands.'

Meanwhile in the east of the county a huge estuary, of which Breydon Water is but a faint echo, stretched inland as far as Acle and isolated the islands of Flegg and Lothingland. It subsequently enabled the Romans to develop waterborne connections with Brundall, near Norwich, and Caistor St Edmund.

The rivers, being unbanked and therefore largely uncontrolled, made substantial inroads into the landscape, much more so than they do today. The Nar, for example, may have been navigable as far inland as Narford. Wandering back and forth over their floodplains the rivers presumably spilled out each wet season, and most of Norfolk's presently well-drained valleys must have had numerous watercourses or at least one major stream.

An additional problem early in the Iron Age was that at the northern end of the chalk ridge, in the Docking area for example, the quality of soil deteriorated because during the Neolithic and Bronze Ages the high lands had been cleared and farmed too heavily. Now the topsoil on the upper slopes was being washed away, causing arable farming activity to diminish or even stop altogether. But woodland clearance, begun in the Bronze Age, continued. Indeed, during the Iron Age the central area of Norfolk was prob-

ably not as thickly afforested as once thought. It seems people were living and working there, for activity has been located in several areas and increasing human activity recorded in, for example, Ashill/Threxton, and on the line of the new Wymondham bypass.

In general climate terms the chilly, wet conditions of the early Iron Age were followed after about circa 150BC by milder weather, until by the time of the Roman Conquest it resembled today's conditions. Later, during the third and fourth centuries AD, temperatures were even higher and the summers were often dry. Then about circa AD400 there was a return to earlier, colder conditions.

But what of Norfolk's north-west coastline, the assumed terminus of the Peddars Way? In recent years the action of sand washed back and forth by storm and tide has scoured away deposits of exposed peat, so that very gradually a landscape built up in the past is being stripped bare and revealed once again, layer by layer. It is within this peat that the original surface used by the builders of the oddly-titled Seahenge (see: A ritual landscape? part one; and later) some 4000 years ago is now being re-discovered. But even this was not necessarily the landscape of the Iron Age and Roman periods, for throughout the centuries since Seahenge was erected the present coastline has changed again from oak forest to sand and saltmarsh. Nothing ever stands still. For example, one estimate of the movement of shingle ridges at Blakeney and Cley puts their landward speed at about one metre a year.

Holme itself was described as a port as early as 1326 when it was ordered to send ships of over 30 tons to join Edward 11's fleet, then assembling in the Orwell estuary before meeting the French. Faden's map of 1797 shows Holme marsh as a curve stretching out to sea, dipping landward again towards Thornham. Holme Scalps, a sandbank on the low water spring tideline, is another feature, this time marginally north-west of the projected line of the old road as it reaches the beach. Bryant's map, published some thirty years later, merely describes the area, somewhat dismissively, as Marram Hills and St Edmund's Point, perhaps combining the location with Old Hunstanton. Again, in 1915 WG Clarke commented that the Peddars Way 'originally reached the coast at some settlement north of Holme, where in Neolithic times the sea-marge was nearly thirty miles northward of the present, a big triangular area having been destroyed by erosion.'

Quite how he reached that conclusion I am not sure - though he was presumably alluding to the North Sea Basin,

Right: A rucksack beside the agger, north of the Thet

or possibly to the known positions of substantial sea banks - but his comments certainly pre-dated the accidental recovery in 1931 of a barbed bone point made from red antler deer which was dredged up between the Leman and Ower Banks some 25 miles north-east of Cromer by the Lowestoft trawler Colinda. It proved humans had penetrated The Ancient Land. In the 1980s radio-carbon techniques gave the point a date of 11,740 (plus or minus 150) years. By the Iron Age the North Sea Basin had been inundated by the sea for several thousands of years. But it does all suggest that Norfolk's north-west coastline did once extend further out to sea than it does today. Indeed, there may even have been a substantial Roman construction of some sort to the north of Holme, for I understand bits of probable Roman (Brancaster-type) stone and other materials have been found in the past on the beach and along the mudflats. Thus we can only speculate on the sites and artefacts submerged and lost, or waiting to be found. As for the Iron Age people who lived in and around the area, well, a little more evidence has been forthcoming in the last few years.

A people on the move

The collection of tribal groupings we now call the Iceni, who inhabited Norfolk, parts of North Suffolk and an island in the Fens, seem to have belonged to those people whom the Greeks and Romans (including Caesar, Tacitus, Cassius Dio and Strabo) called Celts, or Gauls. These tribes spread from the Czech Republic across Europe to Britain and seem to have spoken a language similar to that discernible in the modern Celtic languages of Ireland, Scotland, Wales, Cornwall and Brittany. Quite when this local grouping finally emerged as a recognisible tribe is not known, but they cannot really be perceived as a cohesive entity until some 50 years before the Roman Conquest.

It is possible they may never have been a single tribe, and that after about AD47 a number of local groups simply formed some sort of political and military federation. One shadowy indication of this is the fact that among the eleven tribes who surrendered to Caesar in 55/54BC were the Ceni Magni, possibly the Iceni. Magni (greater) suggests there might also have been lesser sub-tribes, while the names Ceni/Eceni/Iceni might simply represent an attempt by Roman writers to tidy the records. Several of the other British tribes who surrendered, including the Segontiaci, Ancalites, Bibroci and the Cassi, are never heard of again. However, Ecen, as an inscription on coins, and the names Icknield Way, Ken Hill, Ickworth and Icklingham seem to

Above: Military warning sign beside the Way near Thompson Water and inside the Battle Are fence

Left: Pictures from the Prehistoric Society of East Anglia showing the Way prior to 1914/15

Peddar's Way. —1 : South of Thompson Water. 2 : Junction with Tottington Road on Blackrabbit Warren. 3 : Crossing road from Norwich to Thetford. 4 : Intersection of Bridgham Heath Road. (Photos by H. Dixon Hewitt.)

confirm a local area of influence.

During the first century BC the area around Snettisham and Hunstanton may have been a tribal centre for a ruling elite who expressed themselves - and underlined their wealth - in the form of personal adornment and ornate horse and chariot harness and trappings. By the eve of the Roman Conquest, however, there seems to have been an economic and presumably a political shift in tribal focus towards the south and the east, to Breckland and towards Caistor St Edmund, which ultimately became a Roman-controlled capital. Thus it is at least possible that each group had its own leader and that they simply came together under a single leader at a time of crisis, or perhaps because they actually feared or anticipated a Roman invasion.

One reason for the geographical shift may have been a significant increase in population levels, a change reflected in a greater number of known settlements. For example, during the Early Iron Age the people seem to have begun moving west-east across the less hospitable interior regions and to have started the exploitation of the claylands. The Middle Iron Age period saw yet more expansion, but as yet no systematic occupation of the central clays. However, all this clearly changed during the Late Iron Age.

Unsurprisingly, the availability of water helped determine the location of most settlement sites. Early on they were often positioned on the river valley slopes, while the wet valley bottoms were used for grazing. The valley sides were also ploughed, perhaps by oxen, but most of the higher land (the chalk ridge, and Breckland), was of little use for arable crops, so sheep and cattle predominated. In the partially wooded central area, it was pigs.

Villages tended to be groups of farmsteads which grew early forms of corn (emmer, spelt) and barley, possibly for brewing, for beer played an important role in Iron Age life. Winter grain was stored in pits covered by basketwork smeared with clay. The houses were warmed by a central fire, but there was no hole in the roof. Maybe the incessant heat and smoke enabled lichen to grow inside, thus improving the waterproofing. They were also careful and enthusiastic scavengers with a deliberate philosophy of re-useability, for there seems to have been significantly little waste. Many surviving items display signs of having been repaired or reused.

Today, this sounds like subsistence living for the vast majority, but this interpretation need not imply deprivation or poverty. This was a comparatively wealthy agricultural society which loved horses - which they used to pull vehicles - and which was also cleft by strict divisions of class. At the apex of the pyramid, inevitably, was a king, the political and military leader, backed by a warrior class who had sworn loyalty, and a priestly class, the Druids. They were the teachers and astronomers and the keepers of tribal history and folklore who held ceremonies in wild places in clearings or groves, or by rivers and springs, and who still remain a shadowy, mysterious influence. Nevertheless, even in the Iron Age the Druidic movement may already have been ancient and may have gone back hundreds of years, perhaps to the Neolithic.

So on the eve of the Conquest the region we now call Norfolk was a patchwork of small, fertile fields, ditches, scattered settlements, woodland, hedges and tracks, peopled by a mainly agrarian society producing a significant surplus, governed by wealthy ruling classes. Colourful, proud, organised, independent and partially self-sufficient, they may have been more than a little distainful of Roman influence and fashion.

Digging for victory

Norfolk and North Suffolk's Iron Age society, even though it may have been divided into sub-tribes and possibly

Right: Another 1914/15-era picture taken north of Roudham Heath. Note the central rut made by horses

sub-divided politically into pro- and anti-Roman factions, was nothing if not well organised, for a number of construction projects were undertaken which help to emphasise if not that society's strength, in terms of national authority and influence, then at least its wealth and its ability to field large numbers of people for communal work when it was deemed necessary. As a result, enigmatic sites dot the landscape, and they are worth taking into account because of the effect they must have had on the Roman mind.

A good example is the line of forts which arc cross Norfolk in a roughly north to south direction and include Holkham, Warham Camp, South Creake, Narborough and Thetford. Another possibility is an undated ringwork at Bawsey which seems to have been of importance during the Iron Age and was also utilised in some form during the Saxon period. Warham, which represents a staggering community construction input, may well have been built as some sort of refuge.

In Norfolk, most of these sorts of site are classified as 'hill fort types' because in reality, and because of a shortage of actual hills, the builders took advantage of alternative local features such as sloping ground, a river, a sand-spit, marshes, and so on. At Thetford, the fort included an oval-shaped earthwork and two enormous banks and ditches.

The defences seem to have been re-cut in about AD5 in response to some threat or other from the south, which may or may not have emanated from the neighbouring and often troublesome Trinovante tribe. Much later, Norman builders added a motte and bailey castle, in so doing creating the remarkable outline seen today.

It lies on a rise in the curve of the River Thet and over-looked two important adjacent fords where the Icknield Way crossed the river. In fact all of these forts seem to have had some sort of strategic relationship with probable early lines of communication. All of them are also in the western half of the county and seem to reinforce boundaries which, in the Iron Age, may have had a ritual significance, for tucked safely inside the embrace of the arc are the Icknield Way, Ken Hill, Fison Way and Ashill.

Another category of construction - evidently a distinctly Norfolk genre, which may represent a native attempt to replicate the design of a Roman army fort - is a group of enclosures found in North and West Norfolk. They are ditched, rectangular, have a single entrance, enclose an area of about 0.25ha, and were presumably all built for the same or at least a similar purpose. What this purpose was is not clear. Three have been partly excavated, and while not all of them looked defensive, all were probably too beefy to

Over a Norfolk heath
The PEDDAR'S WAY ... near Thompson:

A pen and ink drawing from the collection of cycling artist Frank Patterson, possibly from the 1920s

have been mere cattle stockades. Perhaps they were used as depots.

One of these enigmatic sites, at Thornham, is of particular interest to Peddars Way buffs because it was once held to have marked the location of a Roman beacon sited specifically for the benefit of ferries crossing the Wash; but more of this later. Thornham was a strongly defended enclosure built during the mid-first century AD on the site of an earlier occupation. Another is Warham Burrows, which may date from the Late Iron Age or possibly the Early Roman period. Other examples have been spotted from the air at Heacham, Bodham, Alby, Bintree, Great Massingham and Thetford.

The design of some of these constructions do actually seem to echo Roman forts, raising the possibility that a local tribal member actually saw one and brought back the general idea. Another possibility is that they may have had a ritual fuction. It has been pointed out that rectangular enclosures were regular features of some religious practices on the Continent, particularly in the Rhineland. But it is too soon to be sure.

A further enigma is the linear earthwork known as the Launditch, which may have protected a presently unknown major site. It cuts an east-west Roman road which ran

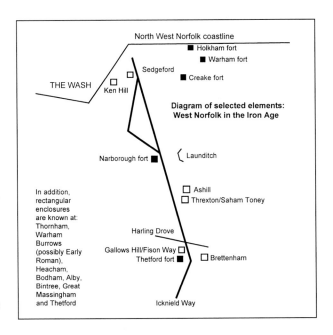

Diagram of selected elements:
West Norfolk in the Iron Age

between Billingford and Kempstone, east of Castle Acre, and seems to have dominated an area between the Blackwater and Scarning rivers. Long thought to have been built during the post-Roman period - possibly at about the same time as other linear systems such as Birchamditch, Fossditch and Panworth - it was re-assigned to the Iron Age when excavation uncovered the fact that the Roman road ran over over it, and not under.

While the Launditch may have been sort some of boundary mark, or even a border crossing, and while the forts may have been defensive or strategic, one still ponders the Druidic influence in some of this.

A ritual landscape? (part one)

It would be easy to fall into exaggeration, to make spurious 'religious' or 'ritual' claims for sites which confound current interpretation. After all, if archaeologists in some far distant future actually excavate the buried remains of Lord's cricket ground, what would they make of it? If a sporting association was not seized upon immediately then I have no doubt it would be pencilled in as having had some possible ritual purpose.

At the same time evidence does seem to be mounting that some parts of Norfolk's ancient landscape, particularly in the north-west and Breckland - mostly close to the present

Right: Approaching Wretham on a damp day

Peddars Way - may have embraced some sort of ritual element. Three sites spring to mind immediately: Seahenge at Holme, Ken Hill near Snettisham, and Fison Way (otherwise Gallows Hill) close to Thetford.

Seahenge has nothing to do with the Peddars Way route, because of its Neolithic dating (about 2050BC), though earlier pre-Roman tracks may have existed in the area. Anyway, about 4000 years ago a mature oak, perhaps blown down, had its higher trunk lopped and tow holes cut, whereupon it was harnessed with ropes made from honeysuckle fronds and dragged on to a low-lying piece of ground. A pit was excavated and the bole inserted upside down with its roots pointing towards the sky. A trench was then excavated around the bole and large timber posts erected to form a solid palisade through which, apart from the occasional crack, there was no way to see through. The only access - visual or physical - seems to have been through a forked post, which had also been blocked.

The original circle was discovered near old peat beds on a presently exposed and eroded portion of the beach at Holme in 1998, and promptly dubbed Seahenge by the media. The structure, inundated every time the tide came in, appeared to comprise 55 oak posts in a continuous ellipse with a maximum diameter of 6.60 metres. It became a subject of great controversy because of the techniques employed, the integrity of the site, its ownership, and even New Age Druidic spiritual considerations, until finally it was lifted by the archaeologists and taken away for examination.

At the time of writing the best interpretation is that Seahenge is a 4000-year-old Neolithic or Early Bronze Age ceremonial or funerary site, probably originally built on land in a 'backswamp' behind a coastal barrier, a location too marginal for permanent settlement. Other features subsequently came to light in the area as the beach continued to erode, including the timbered remains of a raised causeway, pebbles from the beds of small streams and a small piece of wickerwork. Some of the features may have been the remains of barrows or burial mounds. Then in January, 2001, came the announcement that a second smaller circular structure had been discovered, also on the beach.

Seahenge may have been one Bronze Age site in a ritualistic landscape where the sea met the sky, and possibly an area for the disposal of bodies. Or it may have been a spiritual centre. Perhaps there was some echo here of the remembrance of The Ancient Land and the long lost and long-inundated forest. Some societies certainly believed in three worlds - sky, ground, and underground. For example, it was thought that wells or shafts provided a window into the underworld. In which case, perhaps Seahenge's bole was a link between the earth and the spirit world of the sky. Aside from all this, two other aspects of the Seahenge saga were of particular interest, the first being that this was further evidence that the shoreline did once extend further out to sea than it does today, and second, that early tracks may well have lead straight to this landscape of saltmarsh, sky, sea, causeways and enigmatic constructions.

The Seahenge rumpus, by the way, also carried with it faint echoes of an American controversy which followed the 1996 discovery and removal of a human skull (dubbed Kennewick man) near the banks of the Columbia River. The features of the skull, which was about 10,000 years old, were not typical native American, its origin most likely being in the Pacific or Asian Far East. Who was it? Who owned it? Who should care for it? Scientists or tribal elders? Clearly, it had the potential to upset a few theories, and after a great deal of argument and debate the scientists were finally made to hand it back to the local native Americans for re-burial.

A second Norfolk site of particular interest is Ken Hill, near Snettisham. Bronze seems to have become increasingly scarce in about 700BC, and iron began to be introduced, slowly and unevenly, eventually to become the preferred material. Some low grade ores were available locally, the Greensand deposits of West Norfolk being the most important, and two concentrations of iron working settlements seem to have sprung up, one around Middleton, including Blackborough End and Setchey, the other near Snettisham, where specialist smiths produced some remarkable results using precious metals.

Discoveries in the Ken Hill area have revealed more than a hundred torcs (made from twisted bars or wires, and completed with decorated terminals) during the last 50 years. They were probably originally worn around the neck or placed on a statue, possibly as a visual statement of wealth and prestige. Indeed, the classical writer Dio maintained that Boudica herself wore a large torc. There also seems to have been a flourishing trade in precious metals based here, and gold and silver smiths may have produced torcs to order and exported them all over Britain. In consequence, there could even be specialist workshops nearby, still awaiting discovery, a matter made even more pertinent by the fact there was a Bronze Age metalworking tradition in this very same area some 700 or 800 years earlier. So the tradition may have been of very long standing. Indeed, this may have been a votive site with very ancient origins.

Torcs are frequently found in burials and they have been uncovered at a dozen separate sites in the county. But those at Ken Hill were different in that they appeared to have been deliberately concealed or buried in pits, never retrieved and then forgotten, and in consequence lost to the Romans and succeeding generations. A modern coroner's inquest decided they were treasure trove, meaning that whoever buried them had probably intended to retrieve them - a moot point which simply reflects a legal nicety. The present thinking is that they were probably votive deposits, for there were almost certainly religious sites here including, much later, a possible Roman temple.

A 13th century conveyancing document of Newmarket, which related to the Icknield Way, described the old road as going by 'the little hill of the Iceni.' Of course, this hill may have been near Thetford. On the other hand it might refer to Ken Hill. Hill of the Iceni, Ken Hill, Icknield. Were they related in any way? We may never know, but quite clearly something important - a religious exclusion zone, perhaps - was happening hereabouts, for Ken Hill was plainly a key location particularly early in the Iron Age.

As for Fison Way (or Gallows Hill), just outside Thetford, an aerial photograph in 1980 revealed a cropmark covering 4.5 hectares in a field forming the angle between the new bypass and the Mundford road and right beside the line of the old Icknield Way. For three years Tony Gregory excavated what was quickly dubbed 'Boudica's Palace' - though perhaps 'Boudica's Cathedral' might have been a more apt label - which was also adjacent to the find-spot of the Thetford Treasure (a hoard of Late Roman gold and silver jewellery and spoons), and the place where a hoard of Late Roman coins had been found (but not reported) in 1979.

Even though it may have been begun in 200BC, the construction sequence of this curious site climaxed in the early to mid-first century, probably about AD43, with the building of a huge rectangular ditched enclosure surrounded by nine extraordinary rows of fences. Gregory proposed that these lines of closely-spaced timbers, which survived as stains in the subsoil, might have represented some form of artificial grove. The fences were themselves contained within an outer ditched enclosure. Inside, the huge inner space had five circular native-style buildings which faced a massive gateway and 'ceremonial' approach through this strange fenced 'woodland.' There was a marked absence of domestic refuse, again suggesting that the site had a ritual purpose, a specific use, or even a degree of exclusiveness. During the Romano British period another temple was erected about 50 metres away, its enclosure markedly similar to the late Iron Age rectangular enclosures at Thornham and so on, mentioned in the preceeding section. So in getting rid of the major Fison Way structure immediately after the Boudican revolt the Romans must have been fully aware of its sacredness or symbolism.

In possible support of the artificial grove theory, some of the items from the later Thetford Treasure hoard were found to have been dedicated to the native god Faunus, a woodland deity.

This area of Breckland seems to have embraced a number of concentrations of Iron Age artefacts and Fison Way, if not actually the tribal centre of the Iceni, must at least have been a very important focus. It may even have been the spiritual home of the client king, Prasutagus, for it did not appear to have been lived-in and there was no sign of habitation or the remains of luxury goods. Roman military artefacts and other evidence point to the fact that whatever the site was originally used for it was destroyed or at least

Right: A 40mph speed limit on the Way as it approaches Stonebridge; it is actually warning of the road ahead

dismantled by the Romans in the aftermath of the AD61 revolt.

Pagan Celtic religion, saturated by Druidic influences, seems to have been dominated by veneration of the natural, with a particular respect for trees and greenery, animals and birds, fertility and watery places. Even those gods and goddesses who were worshipped tended to be those associated with natural features. Thus islands or promentaries (at the interface of the known and other worlds) were of special significance. Indeed, one noticeable difference between Celtic and Roman worship was that Iron Age shrines were in the open air, whereas Roman religion was generally practised inside. However, the temples were not churches as we know them today, for they do not seem to have been designed to serve communities by providing a place for collective worship, and do not seem to have been surrounded by cemeteries. Rather, the sites and their surrounding areas may have been retained as settings for rituals performed by priests, with the surrounds being kept ritually 'pure.' Perhaps non-priestly worshippers were allowed to visit only on special occasions.

The Iceni also seem to have had some sort of special feeling or reverence for boundaries, while the distribution of pottery and artefacts occasionally hints at careful deposition. In addition, the frequency with which the entrances of Iron Age round houses tend to orientate towards the south-east has also been noticed.

Whether any of this constitutes what might be described or labelled as a 'ritual landscape' remains to be seen. At the very least this and other evidence does suggest that North West Norfolk and Breckland was a very special landscape for the inhabitants over a very long period of time. Early Roman visitors, including traders and the like, must surely have noticed that fact, too.

Doing the business

Trading links and practices in Norfolk are long established. In the Neolithic period flints from the Grimes Graves mines complex, worked and unworked, were being distributed over a wide area, and during the Bronze Age there seems to have been a precious metal workshop in the vicinity of Snettisham. A transportation network presumably developed, too. Exactly the same thing seems to have happened during the Iron Age, but how they organised the distribution and what else was traded is less clear.

Some recycled metals were brought into the region either as finished artefacts or as bullion, while raw materials were

This unusual junction can be seen just beyond Galley Hill, where the hard surface military road leading to the Battle Area sweeps away to the left as the Peddars Way branches to the right

presumably transported by river or by sea, wheeled transport, pack animals or by man. Thus a cat's-cradle of busy tracks and waterways criss-crossed the landscape. The Icknield Way was one of these routes and it may have been marginally more important than some of the others, for most of the sites where Iron Age minting debris has been recognised are either close to the Icknield Way or close to major and therefore probably navigable rivers. Indeed, the two probable minting sites found in Norfolk, at Saham Toney/Little Cressingham, and at Thetford, together with some in Suffolk, seem to underline the importance of transport links in the production of coins.

It is likely that copper and lead ore were also brought in from the upland areas of Britain or even from the Continent, and then exchanged for goods. This intriguing possibility came to light with the discovery some time ago of a wrecked ship off the coast of France. It was carrying roof tiles, and more importantly, lead ingots, 271 of which were recovered. Some were stamped with BRIGANTES, or something similar, and five with ICENES. The cargo may have been on passage between the Continent and East Anglia or Yorkshire, but if the vessel was heading towards mainland Europe then perhaps the Iceni were acting as middlemen. Whichever way it was sailing, a well established maritime trade route thus seems a possibility.

Farm and dairy products were traded locally through local markets, and it is noticeable that during the Late Iron Age, when populations steadily increased, some larger sites seem to have developed from the coming together of groups of smaller communities. Three of these sites, known as oppida, have been located at Thetford, at Saham Toney/Ashill, and at Caistor St Edmund. Other possible large sites include Ditchingham, Crownthorpe, Brettenham, and one other in South East Norfolk, so far not identified. Saham Toney/Ashill seems to have been particularly important, most obviously by AD25, for Robin Brown has recorded suggestions of Iron Age trading in iron (slag fragments) and connections with Dorset (coins). In addition, Watton Brook was then probably a small river, ideal for trading by boat.

Trades and professions? Salt production, timber extraction, charcoal making, iron smelting and clay extraction all seem to have been practised, so they could not have managed without farmers and stockmen, merchants and travellers, charcoal burners and drovers, traders and sailors, river boatmen and boat builders, cart makers and stables, smiths and carpenters and drivers with teams of horses or oxen. If freshly minted coinage or gold torcs were also being moved about the territory, then security guards may have been needed, too.

As for coinage, research suggests it may not have been used, initially anyway, for monetary transactions - bartering was the usual exchange method - but as a handy method of storing wealth. Coins were actually introduced into Britain in about 200BC, though the Iceni seem to have been a little slow off the mark, for the area's first coin seems to have been the gold Norfolk Wolf Type of about 65BC, which depicted a wolf with open jaws and was produced in relatively small numbers. Silver coins were struck later, probably after 35BC, when the production of gold coins seemed to tail away.

It was once thought that some Icenian silver types (boar-horse, face-horse, pattern-horse) represented different tribal sub-groups, but this now seems doubtful. Nevertheless, some Iceni coins do give us the names of tribal heads during the AD30s and 40s, including Anted (which may be a shortened version of Antedios), and in the AD50s, Saenu and Aesu. By far the most common inscription is Ece or Ecen, which may represent a Celtic name for the tribe. The name Prasutagus was also thought to have been recorded, but a recent coin find casts doubt on this. It reads: SUB ESVPRASTO ESICO FECIT and is similar to ESVPRASV

or ILSVPRASV coins from Lincolnshire or the East Yorkshire and Humberside areas, which was a different tribal territory. However, the few hoards which can be dated to the years of the Boudican uprising, AD60-61, tend to be predominantly silver with the find-spots clustered in the south-east of the county around Caistor St Edmund. Whether it indicates that this area may have been one of the focal points of the Boudican revolt is a matter still being investigated.

But before we discuss that, we need to retrace our steps a little.

Tracking an earlier route

There are persuasive reasons for suggesting that the Roman military authorities, in driving the Peddars Way road through Icenian territory, made use of and even improved an earlier route. It is a comfortable solution, and perhaps they did. But for the moment it is an unsubstantiated idea. There is no evidence one way or the other.

In general, the concept of a pre-Roman route is based on the position of known Iron Age and religious sites, the perceived trading instincts of the Iceni - in what was a busy commercial area - and on the closeness of the Icknield Way, which is known to have been not one but several tracks all meandering in the same general direction. So (runs the argument), was the Peddars Way formed partly from an earlier Bronze Age track? Was this early section possibly even a strand of the ancient Icknield Way? WG Clarke lent added force to the idea in 1915 when he said he believed the Peddars Way 'to be a prehistoric trackway adopted and in parts improved by the Romans . . . ' But he did not say how he reached that conclusion.

The picture of Iron Age and Roman Breckland we have today is far from complete, but efforts are being made to bring it into closer focus. As I write, surface collection surveys, or 'forest walks,' are being conducted on 50 re-stocked forest compartments, while earthworks and metal detector specialists are also in the field. So more information is possible shortly.

Meanwhile, there is evidence of pre-Roman routes near Threxton/Saham Toney. Robin Brown writes: "If the stream crossing place was still in use (circa 50BC-circa AD25), and all the evidence suggests that it was, then . . . there would have been a system of trackways leading north and south from this point. To the south, tracks may have gone towards Colchester, Thetford and St Albans, and to the north of Narborough and Warham." There were other probable routes east and west.

Some years ago a Claudian military fort was located by fieldwalking in the vicinity of Watton Brook (see: Fringe activities), the accumulated evidence suggesting it had been occupied by a part-cavalry and part-infantry force immediately after the first revolt of the Iceni in AD47. Later, it seems to have been dismantled and evacuated, and a second, Boudican-period fort, constructed. It is reasoned that the Peddars Way (as it is now called) then came up from the south to reach this fort, though the alignment of the route may have been modified after the Boudican revolt.

Thus it would certainly seem that tracks or routes were in existence long before the Boudican uprising. Again, this is not conclusive evidence of an early north-west to south-east route, but it is hard to believe that there were no lines of communication in this area before the Romans came. In view of the proximity to Saham Toney of other settlements, and the trading inclinations of the peoples of the Neolithic, Bronze and Iron ages, it seems very probable that there were. But it is still not possible to state categorically that the Peddars Way, or some sort of predecessor route, existed before the Romans came. It merely looks as though one might have done.

Right: Vehicle block over the Way near Thompson Water

Fringe activities

What language did the Iceni speak? It seems to have been Celtic, which is thought to have been akin to Welsh/ Cornish or Gaelic/Manx. Because of an absence of written material, however, it is clear a great deal was remembered and passed between generations by word of mouth. Thus a rich legacy of folklore, legend and tradition was gradually built up. However, coin inscriptions in the Late Iron Age indicate the locals may finally have adopted an alphabet, a sort of Romanized writing, or perhaps a Celticised Latin. An early language, however, was trade and commerce, for whatever the state of the English tribal import/export balance sheet traders representing the Roman Empire, particularly from France, seem to have established links with the territory between 100 to 50BC. Main points of entry were on the south coast near Poole (Dorset), and around Essex and the Thames Estuary.

From the evidence available it would seem that inward goods were largely of the luxury variety - exotic items from foreign countries creating new fashions which no doubt appealed to the tribal elite - including wine, olive oil, grape syrups, fish sauce from Spain and table crockery from Gaul and Italy. These were sometimes traded in return for corn, hides, hunting dogs and slaves.

Behind many of these activities were the Trinovantes of Essex, who seem to have been enthusiastic wheeler-dealers. But the trade, and the comings and goings of foreign vessels and crews, and foreign business people, did something else in addition to simply creating a demand for overseas goods. It also helped the English gain some sort of perception of the great Roman power from the Mediterranean whose influence now extended as far as the Channel and the North Sea.

Whether the influence of the Roman traders extended as far as the Wash, or even into some of Norfolk's tidal rivers, is not known, but it does seem that for whatever reason the Iceni were largely unimpressed with much of this new how-de-do. This apparent indifference may have been because of political, economic or even geographical or Druidic reasons. Perhaps they valued their isolation. Perhaps they were suspicious of the implications of an increasingly strong Roman foothold. It is not known. But they do seem to have remained largely aloof from the Trinovantian rush for the New Modernism and the ever increasing flow of exotic Must Have fashions from across the sea.

If the Iceni did indeed see trouble coming then their fears were finally realised when Caesar, maybe attracted by reports of agricultural efficiency and much-needed grain, and accompanied by troops and a fleet, arrived off England's shores in 55BC.

To most Romans, Britain was still a remote, damp, mysterious and misty island on the very edge of empire. In his subsequent writings Caesar mentions a number of tribal groups who sent deputations to meet him, but quite clearly he found the whole project fraught with difficulty. Indeed, after a quick look round he retreated, planned his next move with greater care, maybe gleaned additional information from the traders, and the following year returned with a better equipped fleet and a much larger army.

This time he established a bridgehead on the Kent coast, saw off the local opposition and marched to the Thames. Once across the river he promptly took on the most important of the tribal groupings, the Catuvellauni, under king Cassivellaunus, near St Albans, and captured their stronghold. By now firmly in control, he fixed a rate of tribute (tax) to be paid annually - though whether it was actually paid is another matter - and returned to Gaul evidently satisfied.

If the episode strikes one as a trifle pointless then it has to be remembered it may also have been designed to demonstrate the extent of Roman military might and to dissuade some British tribes from lending assistance to their cousins

The Peddars Way has a rural feel as it passes Shaker's Furze on its way towards Sparrow Hill, Merton, and the Watton road

in Gaul. On the other side of the Channel, of course, Caesar was busily engaged dealing with armies made up of Gaulish warriors and British mercenaries. Again, the two expeditions may also have been sent in to answer a call for assistance from the Trinovantes, forever locked in a power struggle with the troublesome Catuvellauni. There is irony in the fact that within 50 years of Caesar's departure the Catuvellauni, so decisively thrashed by the Romans during the second expedition, got their revenge by taking over the old Trinovantian capital at Colchester.

In the intervening years, when it is most likely trading flourished once again, Roman foreign policy shifted from a desire for annexation to a policy of treaties allied to a careful watch on tribal leaders. But as the Roman traders went about their business so a steady stream of pro-Roman British kings and politicians moved in the other direction, towards Rome, seeking to implore the authorities to intervene on their behalf yet again. Once more, it seems, the Catuvellauni were perceived to be in bullish mode. Caesar's immediate successors, Augustus and then Tiberius, had little inclination towards expansionism, and even if they did consider invading that wretched little country again they seem to have dropped the idea very quickly. In any event there were other things to think about.

A revolt by Florus and Sacrovir in Gaul in circa AD21, in which Druidism was one of the major elements, was quickly suppressed. Very likely some of the priests of this powerful nationalistic cult fled to Britain.

Whatever the provocation, in AD39 the disturbed Caligua finally assembled an army and fleet at Boulogne with the express purpose of crossing the Channel, but for some reason the troops refused to embark. Perhaps the pay was not good enough or perhaps they had heard terrible tales of this strange island. In the event all the generals could do was persuade the archers to shoot their arrows into the sea and the infantry to fill their helmets with seashells. So as not to lose face, Caligua promptly proclaimed a mighty victory over the ocean. Two years later he was murdered. It was left to the scholarly Claudius to make the decisive move. He needed the propaganda of a military victory to strengthen his position and this troublesome little country, rich in minerals, food and raw materials, and the refuge of numberless renegade crackpots from Gaul, was there for the taking. It must have seemed a low-risk enterprise with the potential of large rewards.

The Claudian conquest of Britain under Aulus Plautius occurred in AD43, and he had with him troops withdraw by Claudius from the Rhine and Danube areas. Other than a host of auxiliary troops from garrisons all over Europe, he also had four battle-hardened legions - the 2nd Augusta (from Argentoratum, Strasbourg, initially raised by Augustus); the 9th Hispana (probably from Siscia, Pannonia, roughly, modern Hungary; a pre-Augustinian legion which had served with distinction in Spain and the Balkans); the 14th Gemina (from Moguntiacum, Mainz, known after AD61 as Gemina Martia Victrix); and the 20th Valeria (from Novaesium, Neuss, probably originally raised by Tiberius and after AD61 known as Valeria Victrix).

Plautius and his troops, with clear objectives in mind, stormed across North Kent, swept aside the opposition, and gradually absorbed South-East England into the empire. In fact the advance only halted when it reached Colchester (Camulodunum) where, so confident had they become, they invited Claudius himself to travel to England to receive the submission of eleven tribes. They began the building of a huge, triumphant temple and then withdrew large numbers of troops, leaving behind them a host of retired military veterans and a tinderbox of resentment. Despite warning signs and presumably some misgivings, the 9th was ordered to Longthorpe (Peterborough) and the 14th to Mancetter. And so it was that the Iceni, and therefore Norfolk, became

a client kingdom, which meant they retained most of their own laws and a degree of independence in return for Roman 'assurances' of peace and security. It was occupation by any other name.

Left to its own devices the Roman army quickly began to establish its credentials by building networks of strategic outposts to guard routes and river crossings and introducing an effective system of communication. They rarely let the grass grow under their feet. For example, the partial excavation of a Roman fort at Alchester, near Bicester, Oxfordshire, established that it was probably erected in the autumn of AD44, and may have housed perhaps 2500 legionaries and auxiliaries, some of them possibly archers. The dating of surviving timbers was fairly precise. It meant the Romans were undertaking major construction work in the heartland of Britain within a year of the original landing.

In Norfolk, forts or marching camps were built at Cawston, Spixworth, Barton Bendish, Threxton, Ashill, Swanton Morley, Caistor St Edmund, and Horstead with Stanninghall. Some may possibly date from circa AD47, or from within this four or five-year period, but the general pro-Roman stance of the Iceni suggests little actual military presence was needed. Thus it is at least possible that most of these constructions may date from circa AD60/61. Claudian military units may also have built some of the first roads thus, inadvertently perhaps, setting up an infrastructure which allowed for and indeed enouraged the future development of an expanded network linking the larger towns and villages.

At Threxton, clues as to the siting of a Claudian fort came with the discovery and identification of pieces of bronze military equipment, including coins, harness pendants, buckles, pieces of lorica segmentata (breast armour), a Roman lance head of type used by Gaulish auxiliary cavalry units, and a disc-shaped handle with the name "Primi" (or 'Primi's century') punched on the reverse. It is thought that the fort - perhaps one of a chain along the Peddars Way erected during the aftermath of the first Iceni revolt - was occupied for a short time by a quingenary cohort (500 auxiliaries, part cavalry and part infantry) between the years AD47-58. Interestingly, it stood south of the Watton Brook on a bluff in a field now called Sand Hills, and with a network of tracks and the river ford close to hand it could easily have been in regular communication with the garrison's base at Chelmsford, and possibly with North West Norfolk, too. Meanwhile, other events were stirring which were to upset the uneasy calm.

Above: A walker on the path near Merton

Chapter Two
Revolting natives

THE over-confident Romans were due for a rude awakening, and one incident in particular foreshadowed future events. They had spent the four years since the invasion tightening the noose of control, but in AD47 Aulus Plautius - who subsequently disappeared from the scene, possibly because his wife adopted Christianity, still officially frowned upon - was replaced by Ostorius Scapula, another famous general. He brought with him precise orders from Claudius to press ahead with the complete conquest of the island. This was actually easier said than done. Serious pockets of resistance still remained, one of the most dangerous being Caratacus, in Wales and the West Midlands, standard-bearer of the anti-Roman factions who were, no doubt, also backed by the Druidic hierachy.

In order to advance west Scapula needed a substantial force, and to gather this together and pad out the ranks he had to draw on the local garrisons, which left many of the local posts seriously depleted. Thus substantial tribal areas, particularly in the south-east, had precious few troops to keep an eye on them, or in some cases perhaps none at all. Sensing potential danger, particularly as he and his army would undoubtedly be away for a considerable time, and in order to secure his rear (despite the fact that it did evidently contain a useful proportion of supporters) he evoked the Roman military law the Lex Julia de Armis, which effectively disarmed conquered tribes. It was a stunning miscalculation.

The purpose of the law, naturally enough, was to deprive the tribes of their battle weapons, leaving them with only the right to carry weapons for hunting and while travelling, but not everyone was prepared to accept the indignity. Some must have felt they had earned the right to be trusted, and yet here was Rome treating them like any other lawless people. Others of the anti-Roman faction might have sensed that now was the time to test the mettle of the new man in charge. Either way, the ruling provoked resentment, so much so that in the end a portion of the Iceni, their tempers and patience spilling over, finally revolted.

It was an awkward time for Scapula and his military commanders, with a major campaign awaiting in the west and now a revolt of unknown proportions in the east. But Scapula was not entirely without the means to do something about it. Prior to gathering his army for the campaign against Caratacus in the west, he had the 9th at Longthorpe (Peterborough) and the 20th at Colchester, both within striking distances of the eastern province. In the end he brought together a powerful force, and struck back with indignant fury.

It was then that the renegade factions of the Iceni, apparently with elements of the Coritani from Lincolnshire and the Fens, retreated into a stronghold which, according to Tacitus, was defended by earth banks, ditches and natural fortifications, with a single line of approach along a narrow entrance. This awkward and well thought out configuration made conventional attack strategy impractical, and the wily Scapula, who had included cavalry in his force perhaps in anticipation of a conventional battle, ordered them to dismount. Then he launched a furious frontal attack, on foot. After a bloody struggle the rebels were utterly crushed.

There has been considerable debate over where this confrontation actually took place, for at least two forts seem to fit the description left by Tacitus. One possibility is a fort at Stonea, near March, then an isolated island in the middle of the Cambridgeshire Fens. Again, the description might also fit the fort at Holkham. It sits on the southern tip of some land which stands slightly above the surrounding marshes. The ridge is thought to have been the tail end of an old sand spit perhaps similar to present-day Scolt Head

or Blakeney Point. Then, the sea seems to have stretched as far inland as the present coast road, so there may have been open water, mud flats and tidal creeks between this coastline and the spit. This leaves open the question as to whether access was possible only by boat. In any event, Holkham was well defended, with a bank and ditch along the north edge, facing the spit and the sea, and an entrance on the south side defended by two banks.

Which site was the actual location is one matter. Another is the fact that the result of the struggle was overwhelmingly decisive. A third is the fact that Tacitus made the incident sound very serious indeed. However, lingering thoughts that perhaps it did involve only some anti-Roman elements of the Iceni do carry some sort of weight, for despite the bitterness of the struggle the upset does not seem to have altered the client kingdom status bestowed upon the group as a whole some years before.

As to precisely when the early military guard posts, or forts, sprang into being, it is an open question whether some of them had already been constructed just prior to AD47, or just after, as a means of maintaining a careful watch, or whether the majority in fact date from the Boudican period a decade or so later. Anyway, change was already happening. Before AD43 Britain was peopled by tribal people with

Left: The Peddars Way, looking south, close to the Watton and Little Cressingham road

Below: Dilapidated sign which used to advertise the Lost Nurseries, near Wretham

their own myths and legends. Now they were being sucked into a pagan empire ruled by a 'god emperor.' And to add to the political jigsaw, another important figure had already arrived on the scene.

Enter the pacifier

In the years between the uprising of AD47 and circa AD60 - during which time Iceni territory may have been encircled rather than actually occupied and garrisoned - the Roman army continued to pursue its westward interests, defeating the rebels and pacifying the landscape as it moved forward. Very slowly they forced the rebels, the Druidic priesthood and their followers into Wales, and then further and further north-west. A preoccupied Scapula, now a long way from East Anglia, must have felt confident that with the insurrection of AD47 crushed and avenged, and a new kid on the block in the shape of a pro-Roman Iceni tribal king named Prasutagus, things would remain relatively quiet until he returned.

Tacitus and Dio both mention him in their writings, and yet Prasutagus remains a shadowy, dimly perceived and little-known figure. It is not even known when he first entered the political fray, though it is at least possible he was one of the eleven tribal leaders who surrendered to Claudius at Colchester. He may have come to the fore because of his apparent pro-Roman leanings. Equally, he could have been a puppet king placed in power by the military authorities, or a man the Romans saw as a possible unifying force, someone with the ability to keep the tribal factions in line. Whatever the truth, somewhere around AD47 he seems to have risen to the top of the pile - perhaps at Scapula's insistence - conceivably as head of a new federation of pro-Roman Iceni tribes and presumably after some sort of agreement or accord had been reached. What slim evidence there is merely suggests the existence of a pro-Roman king beginning to break away from Celtic traditions, and even that Roman culture was beginning to infiltrate the royal family and the mint.

Whether or not he was initially put in place by Scapula or one of his predecessors, Prasutagus was a client king, which meant he ruled a client (ie, partially free) kingdom on the edge of empire. Thus freedom from external attack was guaranteed by the Roman army while freedom from internal interference was guaranteed by treaty. Another benefit was exemption from taxes and tributes which otherwise had to be paid to Rome. Inevitably, there was a down-side. In return for all this the king was expected to recognise that he remained in power only by courtesy of the emperor, and what is more, he was also expected to name the emperor as his heir. The theoretical convention was that the emperor would then generously return power to the client king's natural successor. As it turned out, it was a recipe for mischief and misery.

Scapula's military campaigns in the late AD40s, and those of his predecessors, had brought southern England, the Midlands and Wales under the Roman yoke, and so successful had it been that by the time Nero replaced Claudius as emperor in AD54 the one single important exception to the rule was Anglesey, in the north-west corner of Wales. Thanks largely to the efforts of the Druids and their priests it had become a rallying point for resistance, and seems to have continued as a major religious and intellectual centre in defiance of the occupiers. In addition, the last British warriors capable of resisting the Romans were also being drawn to the stronghold.

By about AD60, and with Scapula off the scene (he committed suicide), the then govenor of the province, Suetonius Paulinus, decided to eliminate this nuisance once and for all; and just like Scapula before him, and in order to raise an army sufficient for the job, he reduced the forts and posts to skeleton garrisons and marched off, confident his rear was secure. When the military juggernaut finally

Above: Thorneycroft's heroic 1902 bronze of Boadicea and her daughters, at Westminster Bridge, London

reached the Menai Straits they glimpsed, across the narrow channel, hordes of fanatical warriors and wild priests. It must have been a terrifying scene. But the Romans must also have sensed an opportunity for revenge.

The actual make-up of the army of Suetonius Paulinus at this point is pertinent to the tale, for it is thought to have comprised about 20,000 troops including elements of the 9th Legion (from its fort at Longthorpe, near Peterborough), the complete 14th Legion (from the Midlands, possibly Mancetter), the 20th Legion (Gloucester), and some additional auxiliary regiments. Anyway, a confident Paulinus picked his moment, ferried his men across the channel and ultimately defeated the Druids and their followers after a savage encounter. No mercy was shown, and many old scores were settled.

It was a heady, triumphant moment, and not even Paulinus could have anticipated that storm clouds were gathering and that events were about to take such a turn for the worse that the Roman occupation of Britain was brought to within an ace of being ended. Nor may he have realised there was a woman behind it.

Introducing the queen

Despite the fact that she is Norfolk's first and perhaps best known 'heroine,' surprisingly few facts about Boudica, like her husband, have been gathered. One of the first 'real' people we can actually perceive in Norfolk history, we do not even know when she was born, or where, where or when she married Prasutagus, how many children they had (though two daughters are recorded), or even where the family lived. In truth, the Latin writer Tacitus and the Greek writer Dio Cassius open only small windows on her life, and then on merely a tiny portion of it.

From what is known of the role of women in society during the Iron Age, it seems they were routinely influential and held substantially more central roles than they did in subsequent centuries when their status and authority was greatly eroded, first by Roman and then sometimes by Christian influences. So whereas Roman soldiery might have been astonished at the sight or thought of women politicians, leaders, or even fighters, Iron Age tribal society thought nothing of it. In that single sense Boudica was unremarkable.

Dio speaks of her as a women of 'immense stature,' though this need not mean she was tall by today's standards, though it is always possible she was tall according to the Mediterranean norm. He may have been equating stature with demeanour and authority, rather than with height. But she was evidently red (or auburn) haired and often wore a large golden torc and a voluminous patterned (presumably dyed) cloak and plaid. It would be nice to believe her torc, perhaps a symbol of queenly status, might have had some connection with the Snettisham workshops.

Although Boudica may not necessarily have been born of royal blood, she could have come from the ranks of one of the various Iceni factions or even from a neighbouring tribe, possibly the Coritani, the Trinovantes, or the Brigantes (also led by a woman, Cartimandua). No one knows.

As for her age, perhaps she was not very old after all. She and her two daughters were clearly dreadfully mistreated by the authorities and their representatives immediately before the revolt of AD61, but they may still have been quite young and she herself may have married young. Thus it is at least theoretically possible for her to have been born around AD30 and to have married Prasutagus shortly before or shortly after the first Iceni revolt of AD47. Measured against today's social mores this might have made her a child bride, but one wonders if this was the case in the Iron Age. In any event she was probably aged between 30 and 40 by the time events took a momentous, decisive turn.

Another element of her life not fully understood is the religious dimension which apparently surrounded her. Some writers have gone so far as to suggest Boudica might have been a priestess as well as a queen. As it happens there is an account of her, while addressing her troops, ritually releasing a hare and praying to the god Andraste. But Boudica, the real person, remains as elusive as ever. Even her name has undergone a number of written evolutions - Boudicca, Boadicea, Boudica, to list but three - all of which seem to translate as 'Victory,' the equivalent of the modern Victoria, which undoubtedly contributed to her national renaissance in the mid- and late 19th century.

What does seem clear, thanks largely to subsequent events, is that whatever her rank and status and age here was a woman evidently well versed in current affairs, the ways of battle and military tactics, and the wiles of Roman politicians and authority. At the same time she was also possessed of sufficient influence and charisma to be able to bring together in a common cause - perhaps for the first time - almost the entire tribe, along with anti-Roman supporters from neighbouring tribes, and set them on the path of war against the common enemy.

Where she and Prasutagus might have lived, or had their power base, is discussed next.

Home, sweet home

Some writers, in re-telling the events of the Boudican revolt, have given considerable prominence to word-pictures of the queen and her raggle-taggle, fanatical followers streaming south towards Colchester along either the Peddars Way or the Pye Road, the present Ipswich Road out of Norwich. This is all very well and good, and it certainly presents a tantalising image. But they pre-suppose a number of things. One is that these roads were already in existence in AD61, the Roman military roadbuilders having already done their job before or shortly after AD47. The plain fact is that no-one knows where the revolt first flared, which routes were used by the rebels, or even the location of the place Boudica and her husband called home sweet home.

For a number of years it was felt that Caistor St Edmund and its whereabouts offered the greatest possibility of such a site. After all, the signs of substantial Iron Age settlement in the area had been recognised, and coin hoard depositions dating to around the time of the rebellion added to the feeling that here, or hereabouts, was the heart of the Iceni federation. Another big plus in terms of the theory was the

Right: Reconstructed interior of Iron Age living area (Cockley Cley)

Roman decision to site the new capital there, a ploy which might then be interpreted either as a threat to the dissidents not to misbehave again or as a reward for the pro-Roman factions which did not rise against them. Either way, it does seem logical to suggest the Roman choice of location was a deliberate attempt to subjugate and dominate a former tribal heartland. Again, perhaps they simply liked the site and its waterbourne connections, for life in the township seems to have settled very quickly into a sort of situation not entirely dissimilar from that of the British in India.

But now doubts are beginning to creep in. First, the number of recovered contemporary coin hoards may actually represent nothing more than an imbalance in metal detector useage in and around the Roman township of Venta Icenorum as opposed to other areas. Another reason for doubting Caistor's claims is an increasing impression that, as large as the Iceni tribal presence was in this locality, the intensity of population and the ratio of important sites was even higher over in the west, in Breckland.

There are a number of reasons for thinking this. The presence of the Icknield Way, for a start, and the Peddars Way, which seems to stride ominiously through known Iron

Right: A thriving Iron Age settlement was once sited in the Threxton and Saham area

Age settlements at Brettenham (perhaps a more important site than at first thought, and which may have been a small town), Threxton/Saham Toney (with, as we shall see, its two military forts), and Ashill (where there were ritual well depositions and where fragments of a hacked Claudian statue were subsequently found).

Incidentally, in 1915 WG Clarke recorded that a large number of Roman artefacts including coins, keys, rings and pottery, had been found at Brettenham and that a few years earlier a human skeleton standing upright was discovered in the side of what was then a chalkpit. Earlier still, in 1907, a skeleton and two other skulls along with a spear and part of a helmet were uncovered, leading him to speculate that it might have been the burial place of Roman soldiery. But the essence is that all three places (Brettenham, Threxton/Saham Toney, Ashill) are slowly being reinterpreted as having been considerably more important and more intensively occupied than previously thought. Another factor is an increasing sense of Iron Age activity in and around the parishes of Hillborough, Bodney, Great and Little Cressingham (on high ground above a loop in Watton Brook), Thetford, and along the valley of the Little Ouse. Three of the four known Iceni coin-mould sites are in and around Breckland, too. Then there are the scattered earthworks including a double-ditch enclosure at Barnham, which seems to have been abandoned in the mid-first century AD; the fort at Thetford; and the extraordinary religious centre at Fison Way, which, simply because of its size and complexity must surely must have been a regional tribal focal point.

So perhaps it is towards the Brecks, somewhere around Thetford, that we should look for the power base and home of Prasutagus and Boudica and their daughters. To Brettenham, perhaps, or to Ashill or Bodney, Saham Toney or Threxton, to somewhere in the vicinity of Fison Way, or to some presently unknown site hidden beneath a carpet of pine needles in Thetford Forest. One day, if we are fortunate, the secret will be revealed.

Enter the bad guys

It is possible the blow fell unexpectedly. In AD60, or perhaps just before (but in any event at about the time of the Paulinus campaign in the West Country and Anglesey), Prasutagus died, and it was at this point that the thin veneer of peace which had existed between the Iceni and their neighbours for thirteen years or so finally broke apart.

The wealthy Prasutagus - described as bold or weak, according to one's viewpoint - at least seems to have been a wily operator, for at some point he had evidently attempted, in his will, to retain at least half of his kingdom for his own family by the simple device of leaving only half to the emperor. Under Claudius, of course, he might conceivably have got away with it. But the gamble misfired, and misfired badly, for by now Claudius was dead and Nero was in charge, and he was not the sort of man to allow upstart 'allies' to get away with anything. At the same time various large loans - monies presented to leading British figures by Claudius - were now called in, thanks to the lobbying in Rome of the influencial Seneca, one of the main lenders.

And so it was that the official Procurator, Catus Decianus, seemingly a man with a very thick skin, was sent to the Iceni royal household to enforce Nero's authority by claiming the entire estate. Negotiations quickly became mired and relations soured, presumably because of a reluctance by the Iceni to hand over anything, particularly their ancestral lands. Finally tempers flared with the most awful results.

Whether with the knowledge or nod of the Procurator we shall never know, the widow, Boudica, and her daughters were greviously abused and insultingly treated (including, according to Taticus, rape and physical violence). To rub further salt into Iceni wounds tinpot officials then roamed the kingdom impounding land and possessions. In effect, they treated the Iceni not as allies or as partners - as had been expected - but as defeated natives.

It was this sequence of events, plus another element of urgency brought on by a possible shortage of corn, which helped spark the revolt and which may also explain the presence of Roman coinage in Iceni hoards buried at about this time. But not only the monied aristocracy were affected. As a client state the local tribes were also expected to supply a quota of young men to serve in the auxiliary units of the Roman army, which overnight guaranteed the unpopularity of the law even if it was popular before. Further relish is added to the recipe of mis-management when it is realised that some members of those same families may already have fought against the invaders as mercenaries in Gaul.

Widespread ruination and wholesale discontent beckoned, brought about very largely by blundering, blinkered, thoughtless civil servants and debt collectors.

From a Roman point of view, of course, the civil disquiet could not have happened at a worse time. The army, remember, was several hundred miles away in Wales and Anglesey.

The natives ARE revolting!

The fine detail of the dramatic revolt of Boudica and the Iceni, in which the decisive strings were eventually pulled by the wily and battle hardened Suetonius Paulinus, need not actually concern us too much. A number of books, including my own (Chasing the Shadows: Norfolk Mysteries Revisited), have already mulled over some of the small print, fascinating as it is. However, perhaps the skeleton of this affair does require fragmentary reconstruction if only because of the subsequent impact it had on the tribal lands of the Iceni and, more precisely, on the subsequent behaviour of the military authorities.

When the recently widowed and even more recently injured and humiliated Boudica finally issued a rallying call to the tribes - or when they came to her, which is another possibility - it is clear people responded in their thousands. Among them, it is thought, were members of the Trinovante tribe who, it may be recalled, also harboured particular resentments against the invaders. Other anti-Roman factions may have arrived, too.

Precisely where these key and no doubt emotional tribal meetings took place is not known. Nor is the actual location of the start of the march, if it indeed had a single source. But it evidently began with high hopes of a relatively quick victory. If that year's crops were already planted then the men would certainly have wanted to return by harvest-time. Something certainly drew them on. Perhaps it was loyalty to the queen. Perhaps fifth columnists told them Paulinus and his army had their hands full in the West Country. Perhaps the signs from the gods were good. It is even possible Boudica and her war leaders were boosted by a tribal recollection of the defeat in AD9 of Quintilius Varus and three Roman legions in Teutoburger Wald by Arminius, the Cherusci warleader, which demonstrated that the legions were not invincible after all. Whatever it was, something filled them with hope and confidence.

They must also have realised this was their best and perhaps final opportunity to cast off the yoke and do away with the Roman once and for all. So they met and talked and invoked the gods, and finally they marched, thousands of them, taking with them their waggons, wives and children. Leaving their farms, stock and fields presumably in the hands of the old and those who could not or did not want to fight, they streamed south with Camulodunum (Colchester) on their minds and revenge in their hearts. Alerted to the danger - perhaps by sentries in isolated posts who detected the atmosphere or even saw the approaching horde - a detachment of the 9th Legion, based at

The triple-ditch enclosure near Threxton photographed in 1996. Crop-marks clearly show the cavalry fort dominated Watton Brook (dark line, left) and the Peddars Way (white line, above the modern lane) which entered the fort (left) and continued on top right (farm track, just below the trees). - Picture: Norfolk Museums & Archaeology Service

Longthorpe near Peterborough, under its commander Petilius Cerialis, promptly arranged for messages to be rushed to Paulinus in Anglesey and possibly also to the 2nd Legion based at Exeter, then commanded by Postumus, an elderly soldier on the verge of retirement. Then Petilius moved what remained of his men south-east in a forlorn but desperately brave attempt either to bolster the defences at Camulodunum or to somehow try to slow down the rebel advance. By some means Boudica seems to have anticipated the move, for detachments of her rebels were waiting in ambush. Petilius and his men were caught and his cavalry routed and the survivors hurried back to Longthorpe where, fearing pursuit, they may have constructed a small temporary stronghold.

As leader of the only available Roman force in the area, small as it was - for the bulk of his troops were with Paulinus - it is clear Petilius (and we we shall hear more of him later) acted correctly, but at the same time the remnants of the 9th and their commander were clearly fortunate to have escaped with their lives. Indeed, it is significant that when the ranks of the 9th were ultimately made good after the revolt 2000 new men had to be brought in from the Rhine region.

Whether some of the rebels did actually race to Longthorpe in hot pursuit of the survivors is not known. Even more interesting, perhaps, is the implication that Boudica may have had a reliable tribal intelligence network. Alas for Postumus isolated in his fort at Exeter, rather than commit himself and his troops to a frantic dash across war-torn southern England he seems to have decided to stay put. For whatever reason, the 2nd did not respond to the request for help and therefore did not share the glory of victory. And so, when the revolt was over, the disgraced Postumus did the only thing open to him. He fell on his sword.

Camulodunum, the Roman capital and former tribal centre of the Trinovantes, had been ruthlessly taken over by the military for the express purpose of developing a colonia, a settlement of retired army veterans. In the process, native farmers and townspeople had been brutally exploited. But the Roman township was still under construction and there were no defences. The only defending force, if it could be so described, were the veterans themselves, a sort of elderly Home Guard. Worse still, the only possible place where they could make a stand was the huge and also unfinished classical temple dedicated to the spirit of the dead Claudius. To the dispossessed Trinovantians it was a monument to tyranny, for they had been treated largely as captives and slaves for nigh on a decade.

The town's defensive preparations were also hindered by local agitators so that, for whatever reason, little or no attempt was made to erect barricades or to evacuate the women and children. When the rebels did finally swarm through the streets, burning, murdering and looting, the veterans made their last stand in the temple, fighting gallantly and holding out for two days. But the temple was finally taken and the defenders butchered, the town razed and plundered. In some places the heat from the blaze was so intense utensils melted and ran into puddles of moulten glass.

The horrors and the looting can only be imagined. One of the best known items stolen was a large bronze head of Claudius, evidently hacked from a statue which possibly stood in or near the temple and which was recovered, centuries later, from the bed of the river Alde at Rendham, Suffolk. Interestingly, a portion of the same statue was also found at Ashill, many miles away, suggesting that at least some of the native survivors of the campaign managed to make their way home.

Londinium was the next target for the horde, by now whipped into a frenzy by alcohol, blood-lust, and the Druids. A riverside settlement founded by craftsmen, financiers and traders in about AD50, there was no fort or defences of any sort, and Boudica's bloated mob, probably out of control, levelled it in yet another orgy of violence, filling the sky with screams and smoke.

Poor Paulinus. News of the revolt, which is said to have reached him just as victory was being celebrated on Anglesey, must have jolted him back into reality. He must also have realised that the army's toehold in Britain was in the balance. Being a good soldier he acted speedily and decisively. Ordering the infantry to finish the job against the Druids as quickly as possible and then undertake a forced march towards Londinium, he and a detachment of outriders raced to Londonium to assess the situation. Despite the pleadings of the terrified locals he realised that any attempt at defence of the settlement would at best be a futile gesture and that a set-piece battle was his best chance of victory, when his relatively small but highly disciplined army could at least stand against a huge, disorganised rabble by now drunk on success and a lot more, no doubt. But Boudica was not quite finished, for she changed course yet again and this time fell on Verulamium (modern St Albans), which had to endure precisely the same fate as London and Colchester.

At this moment Roman control of Britain hung on a very thin thread indeed.

End of the affair

When Paulinus and his advance party arrived in Londinium, or at least reached the outskirts, they were in ample time to gain an inkling of what was about to happen. The settlement was in turmoil and panic-stricken traders implored him to defend them and their houses and warehouses. The size of his immediately available force may have numbered hundreds rather than thousands, and it seems he saw very quickly that it could not be defended against the horde. If he committed himself to such a ploy, however tempting, in all probability he would be over-run and wiped out. There was too much at stake for such an exercise. So he made what must be seen as a harsh but tactically sound withdrawal, back along Watling Street, possibly with some of the frightened traders and even Boudica's rebels and their allies baying at his heels. However, and perhaps without ever realising it, the Iceni had just conceded the initiative, because from now on it was Paulinus who was in control of the situation. For the first time since the revolt broke out, he was actually dictating the events.

His withdrawal evidently took him back through Verulamium (St Albans), which was also doomed, back into the Midlands and in all probability back to Mancetter, in Warwickshire, a place he knew (there was an army camp in the vicinity) and which he may already have selected as a potential battle site. Clearly still outnumbered, even if his main force did manage to arrive in time, he nevertheless wanted to face the final, decisive battle on his terms and in a location of his own choosing.

The site of the confrontation has never been precisely located, but at the time of writing the preferred opinion seems to be that it was at or somewhere near Mancetter. Anyway, Paulinus duly met up with the main body of his force, which had marched at speed from Anglesey, and calmly began to prepare them for battle.

According to Tacitus the site in a range of hills offered a clear space in front of the troops and thick woods behind and on either side, giving views of a river and a wide, marshy valley. By the time Boudica and her rag-tag army arrived with their waggons, booty, priests, wives and children, the Roman legions were already drawn up at the top of the slope with the infantry in the centre, the auxiliary cavalry on either side and the auxiliary infantry in reserve. They must have presented a fearsome picture of close, disciplined ranks of steel.

Whether or not Paulinus feared the prospect of prolonged guerrilla attacks penetrating through the surrounding woods

- a ploy by the enemy which might have left him vulnerable - his worries proved groundless. Boosted by success after success, the Iceni seemed quite prepared to gamble everything on one battle, one final glorious gesture.

In the end Boudica was left with no option but to mount a frontal attack, which is precisely what the Romans wanted them to do. Pausing only to move their baggage train into a semi-circle behind them, so that the spectators had the best view, the rebels then began to advance over the swampy ground and up the slope. Then two flights of Roman javelins whistled through the air, causing confusion and casualties, and on the soft, wet ground the attack faltered. The first doubts appeared and Paulinus, sensing the hesitation and seizing the moment, ordered his legions forward down the slope. This time Boudica and her troops were not prepared, and they were forced further and further back. The rebels panicked and some began to run, but now they were trapped and hampered by the baggage train, and in the confusion the legions and their auxiliary support relentlessly hacked and slaughtered everyone within reach. When a few rebels tried to run they were cut down by the waiting cavalry. Ultimately, the Roman victory was complete. Taticus (Roman, of course) said 80,000 Iceni and their allies were killed at a cost of 400 soldiers, and implied that the British fielded perhaps 200,000 men against 10,000 legionnaries and perhaps a similar number of auxiliaries. All these figures have to be taken with a pinch of salt. But it does seem to have been an overwhelming defeat for the Iceni, who left most of their number dead or dying on the field. What few survivors there were had to slink away and flee for their lives. Boudica, so later Roman writers inferred, survived the battlefield but lost her life shortly after, probably from taking poison. To all intents and purposes the blood spilled at Mancetter marked the end of the Iceni, who were never to be heard of again, and the end of the Iron Age. In any event, the fate of Britain for the next 350 years was settled that day.

Interestingly, excavations in Fenchurch Street, London, where the layers of burned material from the time of the Boudican attack were between three inches and one foot thick, other evidence suggested that although the Romans were initially forced to abandon London, they returned almost immediately after the battle. What is more, they also appeared to have hurridly built the settlement's first town wall. It was a one and a half-mile system of double ditches and banks topped by timber palisades, some of the timbers of which were charred and presumably salvaged from the wreckage of the conflagration. But in essence it was a strongly defensive arrangement which suggests the military authorities may have been far from convinced that, despite Mancetter, the revolt was completely over.

Perhaps the wall can be put down to traditional military thoroughness. On the other hand, maybe bands of rebels were still roaming the countryside, something which might also go some way to explaining the presence of other emergency fortifications at Longthorpe and even the construction of at least one large cavalry fort in Norfolk.

Very hot pursuit

What did actually happen to Boudica? She is said to have departed the battlefield, alive, only to die some time later, possibly by suicide. But nothing is known of her movements or intentions. Nor, despite the best efforts of numerous legends and tales, and a wealth of folklore, has the site of her final resting place (what a find that would be!) been located. In fact there are two mounds in Norfolk with legends or names linked to Boudica. One is Boadicea's Grave or Soldiers' Hill at Garboldisham Heath, beside the A1066. The other is Vikings' Mound or The Bubbener - which may be a corruption of Boudica - at nearby Quidenham. Alas, there is no evidence to confirm a connection.

Quite simply, she would have had few options left and yet may have been perfectly aware that the Romans would exact a very heavy price for the rebellion. So she may simply have tried to return to her homeland, or even tried to find a bolthole in the Fens. In consequence, she may lie in a hurridly dug grave in some long forgotten grove.

On the other side of the fence it did not take many weeks for Paulinus to make good his battle losses, for he hurridly shipped in reinforcements from Germany including legionaries, eight auxiliary infantry cohorts and two auxiliary cavalry regiments. To add weight and conviction to the inevitable policy of retribution, and as a means of providing extra support for the troops in the field, a new military base was built at Great Chesterford (Essex) along with bases in Suffolk, probably including Pakenham, Coddenham and Stuston. Norfolk, of course, was not immune from the creations of the military working parties, and new camps sprang up here, too, at Threxton - of which more later - Horstead, Worthing and possibly Caistor St Edmund.

It was a massive operation, and it is even possible the 9th Legion - no doubt thirsting for revenge after their cavalry was ambushed by Boudica early in the campaign - together with other elements (possibly the 14th and 20th, plus auxiliaries) was one of the units given the task of mopping

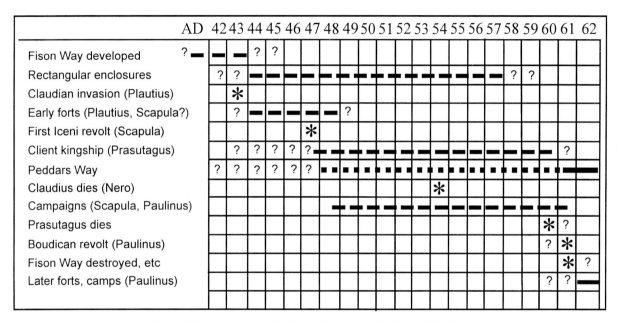

Possible sequence of selected events, AD42 to AD62

up the survivors of Mancetter and destroying whatever or whoever else was left. They probably relished the task. Old scores were there to be settled as local tribal life was systematically destroyed, a task evidently pursued with thoroughness, and one which may have spilled over into a second year as the troops are known to have stayed 'sub pellibus,' meaning they over-wintered in their regulation leather tents. Of course, the comment might also imply that the campaign of punishment did not actually begin until quite late in the year.

Those panic-stricken survivors who still had tangible wealth buried their secret nest-eggs (usually coins and precious metals) if and when they could, though many never returned to claim them. Villages were destroyed, crops (if planted) and livestock wiped out, and Boudican sympathisers hunted down.

Oddly, no layers of charred debris have been found in Norfolk, as they have in Colchester, London and St Albans, which is a little difficult to understand. But the effect was the same. The economy was destroyed, the Iceni leaders were dead or scattered, farms abandoned and homes razed. Inevitably, starvation stalked the land. In London, in Boudican burnt layers, the remains of imported grain from from the Mediterranean has been found, suggesting there

might have been a number of poor harvests in the south of Britain. A grain shortage on the eve of the revolt might therefore have contributed to pre-rebellion tensions. Now, however, it must have spelled total disaster.

In another move probably designed to tear the heart out of the Iceni, the Fison Way site, a major location probably at the heart of Prasutagus' power base, was either destroyed or systematically dismantled. Hundreds of timbers from the nine-deep rows of fences were deliberately carted away, either by the military or by military controlled work gangs. Perhaps the army was concerned by site's defensive possibilities; or they wanted to take over a strategic location (it was beside the Icknield Way, and enjoyed commanding views of the local landscape); or perhaps they simply wanted the timber. Yet another possible reason, of course, would be revenge and sheer bloody-mindedness.

Basically, Fison Way represented a huge supply of timber. If its rows of stakes stood six feet high, then it has been calculated there must have been at least 70 running miles of timber. Anyway, pieces of military equipment including hinges and buckles from a breastplate have been found there, but again, there was no sign of rotting or burning in the postholes. The structure simply disappeared.

It would be interesting to know if the Romans did actually

try to maintain some sort of balance in the midst of all this destruction, for it has to be remembered that some factions within the Iceni tribal structure may not have joined in the revolt. Again, Paulinus knew he must seek retribution. The revolt could not pass unpunished. So on one hand there was a need for the rebels to be punished and their culture destroyed, and on the other the need to retain an ability to pay taxes.

The hated Catus Decianus, presumably appalled by the carnage sparked by his blundering incompetence, is said to have fled to France, and he was soon replaced by Julius Classicianus, who assessed the situation and began to express his concern at the level of destruction and the vengeful cruelty of the army. Gradually, Classicianus took on the role of peacemaker, and finally reported to Rome that the hard headed Paulinus, who showed little sign of softening his stance, was the real problem. The military commander eventually became the subject of an official inquiry instigated by Rome and headed by a Greek ex-slave and civil servant, Polyclitus. The upshot was that despite the undoubted courage and skills he displayed as a military commander, Paulinus was conveniently retired. His replacement was yet another conciliator, Turpilianus; and his successor as Procurator, in AD63 through to AD69, was

Trebellius Maximus, also known for his expertise in dealing with aggrieved provincials.

The administration of Maximus seems to have been courteous and conciliatory, and not until AD71 and the appointment of Petilius Cerialis (remember him?) was there a resumption in the wars of conquest in western and northern Britain, this time under the new Flavian dynasty. By then, however, the Iceni were destroyed and the Iron Age was at an end. As a small footnote it is worth relating that the efforts of Classicianus the peacemaker were remembered, however. When he died his widow, Julia Pacata, commissioned a rather fine tombstone, fragments of which still survive.

The view from above

In 1996 an aerial photographic sortee which enjoyed the privilege of being in exactly the right place at precisely the right time, and in perfect weather conditions, confirmed a earlier suspicion that at Threxton/Saham Toney there was indeed the cropmark of a large Roman cavalry fort. It was a significant find. This extensive construction had been erected close to where the Peddars Way crossed Watton Brook, for in the resulting photographs the Way was clearly visible running across Church Meadows and then, on the west bank of Watton Brook, continuing through the southern entrance of the fort and out the other side. The road looked to be about 10 to 15 feet wide, which is narrow for a military road, but it is possible this was simply the surviving metalling, the agger having disappeared.

The fort also seemed to boast three ditches, two of which were probably palisade or rampart trenches, while a third might have been an open defensive ditch, a useful requirement against Iceni horsemen. The site may also have boasted a special annexe for horses. In any event the fort had the usual distinctive 'playing-card' corners and a clear and strategic relationship with the Way, and an immediate conclusion was that it had been built at some point in the AD60s possibly as a key element of the military campaign to suppress the Boudican revolt and to add sinew to the swift and repressive aftermath.

It also raised the interesting question of whether, in light of the defences, some sort of resistance was still being carried on and if the troops were subject to, or even expected, sporadic attacks from roaming bands of survivors or mauraders.

On the other hand, such a large requirement might simply have been ordered on a 'just in case' basis.

Whatever the interpretation, the 14-acre fort sprawled across the corner angles of four separate fields and over a road, and clearly incorporated the Way after it crossed the Brook. This was a strategic location because it not only controlled the intersection of two routes (the Way, and an east-west road through Watton), but also the river crossing. It also had access to communication routes south to Brettenham and thus to legionary bases at Chesterford and Colchester, and north, possibly to Castle Acre.

There is no doubt that this Threxton/Saham Toney site, and in particular this part of the Way, seems to have been at the forefront of Roman military activities in Norfolk. Fieldwalking evidence confirms the presence of an Iron Age/Icenian community close to the river crossing which may have developed into a civilian village centered on the fort and, after the soldiers had gone, into a small market town.

The earlier fort, which has never been visible on aerial photos, evidently sat on the higher ground south of Watton Brook, dominating what may have been the only crossing place between Carbrooke and Bodney. In the middle of the larger cavalry fort, however, the Way became part of the Via Principalis, or main thoroughfare, for the fort it seems to have conformed to the traditional T-shape pattern of streets. Interestingly, it was not quite symmetrical in that one diagonal frontage was deliberately faced south to dominate the river crossing and Way to the south.

There is no evidence at the moment for gates on either the north or east sides, but there may have been one to the west, leading to the north-west continuation of the Way. Travellers from the south, sidetracking the earlier, smaller fort, would therefore have crossed the Brook by a causeway, or possibly by a bridge, and entered by a guarded entrance. From the Via Praetoria they would have turned left at the T-junction inside fort on to Via Principalis, and then ridden out of west gate and turned roughly north towards the coast.

Right: Where the Way passes the remains of the ruined railway bridge, north of North Pickenham

The whole site as seen from aerial photographs has a feeling of solidity about it, and it remains stunning evidence of the importance of the location. Estimates suggest it was probably large enough to have accommodated 800 to 1000 men, possibly several military cohorts (a mixture of infantry and cavalry). Even so, found coinage suggests it was occupied for two years at most, and probably less. Then, with resistance at an end and the job done, the troops no doubt dismantled the palisades and marched off. It is thus possible it was intended only as a temporary base, with no substantial buildings and with the men living in tents or wooden barracks. To Robin Brown, confirmation of the presence of the cavalry fort underlined his belief in the immense importance of this locality. In a letter to the author (July 26, 2001) he writes: "The fact that the Romans built two forts (at this site) suggests to me that the impetus for both revolts (AD47 and AD60/61) came largely if not principally from here. The coin evidence supports this . . . The Peddars Way was a convenient main road leading south to Colchester for Boudica's horde to travel along."

Military theory and dating

The Peddars Way, unlike the so-called Pye Road (from Venta Icenorum to Scole and beyond; otherwise, the modern A140), has no obvious destination. While the Pye Road tended to travel in a number of short, straight alignments, however, the Way seems to have taken a more purposeful route for much greater distances. In other words, the Pye (named after the Magpie Inn, incidentally, which dates from the 18th and 19th century coaching era) took a more leisurely approach, suggesting it may have been built for civilian and administrative purposes. Set against this the Way looks like an early military road, built in a hurry to get somewhere in a hurry.

Of course, not everyone has agreed. WG Clarke pointed out that 'no part (of the Way) seems absolutely straight; it winds more or less according to the nature of the country.' This is something the hiker and stroller can confirm. At the same time, and aside from numberless minor local adjustments, many of which are probably post-Roman additions, the 14-mile stretch from Shepherd's Bush to the Ringstead road - other than its uncharacteristically tortuous approach to the Heacham river at Fring Cross - is more or less straight. Other features suggestive of a military origin are the road's size and shape, which certainly give the overall impression of having been on a greater scale than many fellow roads in other parts of the county.

If still more evidence is required then there is the road's

direction and course. The actual route seems to have been identified a long time ago. For example, WG Clarke said its course was correctly recorded by Samuel Woodward in 1830 (and written up in Archaeologia, vol 33, page 361, though I have not seen a copy in order to verify this), and even marked on Ordnance Survey maps of circa 1915. Some writers, however, still insisted on adding variations of their own ('the road from Brancaster to Swaffham'; 'the road from Brancaster to Castleacre, Swaffham, Ickborough, Brandon, and thence to Exning, Bishop's Stortford and Stratford-le-Bow'; for example).

But the fact remains that in Norfolk, and once over the Little Ouse ford at Knettishall, the road ran through or not far from Brettenham, the Fison Way/Gallows Hill ritual site, the Icknield Way fords at Thetford, Threxton/Saham Toney, Ashill, Panworth, Castle Acre, Fring, and Ken Hill and beyond. Significant sites all. In other words, it sliced like a dagger through the heartlands of the Iceni.

There is another factor at work here, too. It may be important that the settlements of Brettenham and Threxton/ Saham Toney are the only places of significance along the road's Norfolk length which actually survived into the Romano-British period. And only Threxton/Saham Toney (which became a crossroads settlement, one branch of the east-west route following an alignment through what is now Watton High Street and along the town's Norwich road) seems to have been a place of any size. Castle Acre, other than its crossing place over the Nar, seems to have been a later, largely Norman development.

So in view of an apparent lack of large settlements along the line of the Way it is again difficult to argue against the expectation that, initially at least, the road was born out of simple military necessity.

Another possible underlining of the military influence in road building in general can be found in the ancient field systems of South Norfolk and particularly in the Dickleburgh area. Here, the Roman Pye Road cuts across the fieldscape at an angle, and was clearly imposed, regardless of what was the road's purpose or in its planned path.

All in all, the inescapable conclusion at the moment is that the Peddars Way was a road - maybe in parts even a replacement road - laid down either by the military themselves or by labouring gangs working to military orders, or to military specifications. Which still leaves the problem of dating.

One hypothesis has been that many of this country's military roads were laid down as part of a 'rolling programme,' meaning that the construction work was part and parcel of a military advance, and completed at the same time. There is also a suspicion that soon after the Boudican revolt, and possibly as a military response to it, they built some short stretches of road purely to facilitate patrol and lookout duties. Indeed, the Haggard's Lodge road which runs from Egmere to Barwick may well fall into this sort of category. It is possible some sections of the Way may have been used for this purpose, too.

Whatever the truth, it would seem that during the early years of the occupation road construction was a military responsibility. The first surveyors were probably military surveyors. In fact, some commanders may even have persuaded their troops that the building of roads was an honour, or a solumn duty, for at least one dedication found in Catterick was 'to the god who invented roads and pathways.' It is not an unknown concept. Medieval benefactors were regularly persuaded of the spiritual mileage and local kudos to be gained in paying for the building of bridges, causeways, or other highway improvements.

At the same time, and from what is known of the years immediately after the Boudiccan revolt, military concerns and a military requirement for roads in East Anglia, and in Norfolk in particular, seems to have faded very rapidly,

perhaps even within two to three years. Quite simply, the threat of further trouble seems to have evaporated very quickly. The local situation stabilised and the troops were needed elsewhere.

The dating and sequence of construction of these early roads - or indeed, almost any of the Roman roads in Norfolk - is not known, but core work on the network may well have been completed during the second half of the 1st century AD. Nor is it known when planned road construction work actually began in the area.

Some writers have suggested that the southern end of the route (for example, Long Melford to Ixworth, and its extension, which headed towards Crownthorpe) might possibly have been built in the AD40s or 50s, while the Peddars Way extension might have been added immediately following the Boudican revolt. The Fen Causeway, some think, is 'perhaps Neronian,' which would make it post-AD54, or possibly AD60/61. Another writer has suggested that the road north from Coddenham has been dated to about AD70, which ties in with the circa AD70 dating for the main street grid within the township of Caistor St Edmund.

All of which surely means that the military roads were earlier rather than later in the scheme of things. In consequence one possible date, bearing in mind the likely need for a military presence, might have been shortly after the invasion of AD43. Of course, there were more pressing military needs elsewhere, and the land of the Iceni might have been viewed at this time as largely pro-Roman, or at least grudgingly co-operative. Another possible start-time date is immediately after the AD47 rebellion, when troops may have been much more active and present in much greater numbers. Yet another potential date is AD61/62, immediately following the Boudican revolt, or at about the same time the decision was also being taken to site the regional administrative capital at Venta Icenorum (Caistor St Edmund). A purely civilian - as opposed to military - administration for the region might have been in place by circa AD75 by which time, one supposes, a useable network of roads was already in being.

So AD44 to circa AD65 seems the likely start-time slot, a narrow circa 20-year period which may have seen gangs (first military, then possibly civilian) working their way across the Norfolk landscape on a construction programme the scale of which would not be seen again until Victoria was on the throne and when the railway network began to snake across the countryside.

Right: Procession Lane, near North Pickenham

Building bridges (and roads)

It seems likely that Paulinus had under his command at least two legions whose expertise and experience in constructional work was such that it was still being called upon by the military authorities decades later. For it remains a fact that the 20th was subsequently employed on Hadrian's Wall (circa AD122-150), and the 9th on the Antonine Wall (circa AD145-158). Building work, including the construction of roads, would have been as second nature to them, for the Roman soldier was quite used to carrying 50lb as he completed the day's march, and then digging defensive ditches before he was allowed to eat and turn in for the night.

They were very efficient engineers. Where roads had to cross wet or marshy land, or even river flood plains, as at Thorpe Farm, they sometimes raised them up on corduroy timber causeways, one of which was excavated at Brampton in the 1970s, or simply placed them on a bank, known as an agger. In later centuries this technique may have given rise to the still familiar name, High Street, which in turn came to signify Important Street (otherwise, one raised in importance above the others).

They clearly had a variety of approaches to deal with particular problems. For example, one section of the Fen Causeway was lifted up on a foundation of oak trunks, branches, wattle, stones, and up to 3ft of gravel aggregate. At Scaftworth, on the Nottinghamshire and Yorkshire border, a unique timber and turf road was excavated in the 1990s (Current Archaeology, No 151, February, 1997) at a point where the Lincoln to York road crossed the river Idle. Alder, willow and poplar had been used and tree trunks placed as three parallel 'rails,' with smaller stems positioned at right angles and brushwood and turves placed on top. This construction was clearly built in a hurry in the circa AD70s, and it was ultimately replaced by a more conventional highway.

The Peddars Way as we see it today crosses several waterways including the Heacham river (Fring), the Nar (Castle Acre), tributaries of the Wissey (North Pickenham and Threxton) and the Thet (East Wretham), the Thet again (Thorpe Farm, where it is known as Droveway Ford) and the Little Ouse (Knettishall, at Blackwater Ford). Nationally, a pattern can often be seen in Roman endeavours, thus: wide rivers sometimes meant anchored flat-bottomed boats, and planks; deep rivers required trenches cut into floodplains to lower the water levels; while smaller rivers were occasionally crossed by temporary plank bridges set on piles.

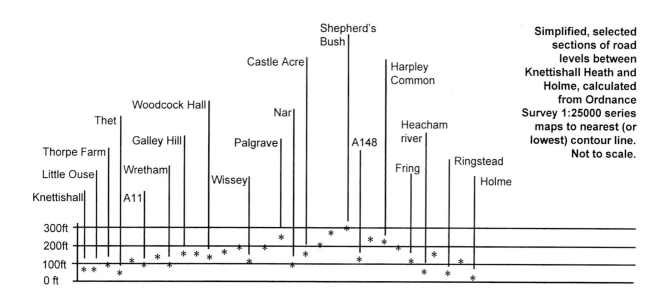

Simplified, selected
sections of road
levels between
Knettishall Heath and
Holme, calculated
from Ordnance
Survey 1:25000 series
maps to nearest (or
lowest) contour line.
Not to scale.

Interestingly, when the line of the Peddars Way was trenched some years ago by excavation equipment prior to the building of the Swaffham bypass, no sign of Roman work or even a profile of the road was discovered. Faden's map (1797) at this point shows the two lines of the Peddars Way slightly off-set from each other, part of the distortion perhaps being caused by a tollhouse which was established on the north side of the main road between the two crossing points. One guess is that centuries of agricultural activity had changed this crossing long before. On the other hand, not all sections of road were built with a metalled surface and side ditches.

In other words a wide range of options were available to the engineers and surveyors. At one end of the scale were the impressive military roads, some (though not in Norfolk, as far as is known) surfaced with cobbles or stone blocks. At the other end of the scale most roads, particularly in rural areas, seem to have been little more than unmetalled tracks. The lesson is that most roads were built for a specific purpose with specific objectives in mind. Others, including pre-invasion Iron Age tracks still in use during the Roman period, came into being spontaneously (homestead to livestock paddock, paddock to grazing grounds, settlement to market, for example), perhaps to be confirmed by

hardening or metalling at a later date and as travel volumes increased.

Again, if the military and their surveyors were involved in the development of the early phase of the local network, as they appear to have been, then native work gangs or even local contractors may have been employed. Individual gangs may even have been responsible for particular stretches. On the Peddars Way, for example, an unevenness in construction methods suggests that different gangs may well have been used, for marginally different specifications seem to have been employed, the final decisions, as ever, being based on the availability of local material and the likely category of use of a particular section. Most roads seem to have been built for non-military purposes.

The surveyors - military men or not - must also have possessed a remarkably detailed working knowledge of the landscape through which the route was passing, which in turn begs the question of whether they had maps, whether they surveyed ahead of the work gangs, or if they simply gleaned their information from locals or traders. One example is the clever use of a tongue of land where the Fen Causeway emerges from the fen at Denver. In general terms, their roads seem to pay careful regard to potential or real obstacles, and in consequence they are not always perfectly straight. Mostly they chose the shortest practical route. As for the general straightness often associated with Roman roads, this is thought to be a result of careful surveying and sighting from one high point to another, or at least from positions with extensive fields of vision. Sections of existing pre-Roman tracks may also have been pressed into service. After all, practicality was the essence. Thus the Peddars Way gives a strong impression that it skirted the edge of the central boulder clay plateau (to the east) and the sea and the Fens (to the west) and in general hugged the upper reaches of the chalk ridge, slightly to the east of today's accepted Icknield Way line. It would have provided a speedier and more direct route to the coast than the meandering early tracks, and offered a greater degree of purpose and watchfulness. This can be construed at least two ways. It may have been a fast, high profile route, built to impress and intimidate. Or its higher profile may have reflected a careful, watchful outlook. Without wishing to over-cook some rather thin ingredients, the planning of the Way may have included elements of both.

The physical side of road building was more straight-forward. Once a line had been determined a strip of land on either side was cleared and parallel outer ditches, or markers, were sometimes ploughed or dug. A centre line may also have been marked, gouged in the topsoil. The inner core of the road was then built up using material scooped from a second line of inner ditches, dug for drainage, and which also defined the road's final width. Once the inner core and scoop ditches were complete, then local material (in Norfolk, gravel, flint, crushed stone, chalky clay) was used to build up the agger (the embankment which carried the road) which was then cambered and metalled with small stones or gravel. All this was done, it should be remembered, across a landscape already littered with homesteads, settlements, fields, farms, hedgerows, routes and tracks. But of course, conquering heroes did not require planning permission.

Some aggers were between 8ft and 50ft across, the larger ones presumably for lines of passing traffic. In fact the Peddars Way today displays a bewildering variety of widths, though it has to be remembered that not all measurements are based on the same rules (do you measure from ditch to ditch, and if so, from which side of each ditch?; and where do you measure from if the drainage ditches no longer survive?), while some sections of the Way we see today may not accurately reflect the Roman original. Centuries of farming and wear and tear, and centuries of local modifications, must have distorted and altered the image to a substantial degree.

What some of the measurements do is confirm a general unevenness in the construction of the road, suggesting local amendments as opposed to an overall specification. For example, on one section of the Way near Bircham I once measured out 16 paces (about 45ft) from hedge to hedge, though this width may have been distorted by parish boundary ridges, nearby farmland, or even by the hedges themselves. On the other hand, 16ft has been recorded at Brettenham and 36ft at Bridgham Heath. In 1915, according to WG Clarke, the Way at Fring was 20ft from bank to bank with the centre of the road two feet above the side level. He also pointed out that 'on the northern part of Roudham Heath it has a dry ditch on the west and a bank on the east, with a width of 17 paces, though in various portions of its course its width varies from 20 to nearly 40ft.' The recorded widths of some Suffolk roads include: Barningham Park, 45ft (on the line of the Peddars Way, measured by Jonathan Mardle in the 1950s); Long Melford, 22ft; Pakenham, 30ft; Icklingham, 24ft; Coddenham, 32ft; and Rattlesden, 15ft. And so on.

One of the best surviving pieces of Peddars Way agger in Norfolk is south of the river Thet at Brettenham (Thorpe Farm) where it forms the western boundary of the Thorpe Woodlands camping and caravan site. There is another short section on the line of the Way north of the plantation north of the Brettenham-Bridgham road. A few yards into Suffolk, there are also faint traces of an agger in the trees near Knettishall's homely little National Trail car park. Excavation at Brettenham in the 1930s, which endorsed the 16ft measurement, also found the road was 2ft 6in high in the centre and built of rammed flint topped with gravel. On the east side of the Brettenham road a gravel pavement, or layby, continued for a further 4ft. North of the river Thet the agger was built largely of rammed chalky flint and boulder clay. Special conditions may have applied here, however, because of the proximity of a settlement and an unencumbered river which must once have moved back and forth across a substantial flood plain.

Incidentally, at the southern (Suffolk) end of the Way's continuation route towards Colchester there are at least three places called Stone or Stoney Street, perhaps reflecting the nature of the route's former surface.

It has to be said that in Norfolk military surveyors exploring the local landscape would have been faced with a comparatively easy task, the county's section of the road rising very gently from below 100ft at the Little Ouse and Thet river crossings to a mere 302ft or so at Shepherd's

Bush, before falling once again to sea level.

Of course, bridges were expensive, took time to build and were vulnerable to attack, so logic suggests that early on at least they preferred to incorporate useable fords and traditional crossing places. Presumably this was the case at the Little Ouse, and possibly at the crossing of the Thet. Indeed, the only location on the Norfolk line of the Peddars Way where it is currently thought there might have been a bridge is Threxton/Saham Toney, over the Watton Brook - which would have linked the road and the second Roman fort - where traces (timber baulks) of a construction, or perhaps a causeway, have been found. Much further west, an excavation in 1933 did come across evidence of a possible timber bridge at Downham West which once carried the Fen Causeway across what was once a stream and then a rodden (the silted remains of an extinct watercourse).

The Romans are thought to have built over 8000 miles of roads in Britain and it is unlikely they would have placed milestones or markers everywhere. Indeed, only about 110 have been discovered in the country, dating largely from later rather than early periods of the occupation, and usually in areas which had local quarries. It is not known if mile markers were provided on the Way, though there are two or three enigmatic documentary references to large stones at Ickburgh, Grimston (in 1588, known as the Rome Stone) and (in 1740) between Threxton and Saham Toney. It was said that two stone column bases found some time ago at Downham West might have supported mile markers, but this seems unlikely. Stone in Norfolk was too valuable for such a use, so perhaps they came from a high status building or were reused as ballast on a Roman barge on a fenland canal. But no actual milestones have been unearthed in Norfolk. Suitable local stone was probably not available, and if wooden mile markers with painted numbers were the norm then they would have decayed a long time ago.

At the heart of all this conjecture are the questions of who built the roads and when, and how long it would have take them. More precisely, how long did it take to build Norfolk's stretch of the Way?

The most likely candidates as builders are the 9th Legion, who were based at Longthorpe from AD45 to 65 and who were then (to AD71) moved to Lincoln. But a large dollop of guesswork is required on these matters. One experiment in the 1980s, based on 1000 military men working 10 hours a day, found that construction time varied greatly according to ground conditions (swamp, forest, heathland, grassland).

But it concluded that a basic military 'service' road between Richborough and London (Westminster), a distance of about 120km, could have been completed in about 15 weeks. On this basis, a similar 'service' road from Knettishall to Holme (about 46 miles, or 72km) might have been finished inside 10 to 12 weeks.

However, this is hardly relevant to the finished design of the Way which included sequences of ditching, metalling, and the building of aggers, and which was evidently a substantial highway built in the expectation of heavy use. Would this have taken five times as long as a 'service' road? Another estimate has it that military men could build a mile of road in three or four days. If so, and assuming the existence of a rolling programme, then the Way may have taken seven months to build. This, it has to be remembered, would have been achieved while working in an inhabited landscape and surrounded by a sullen population. It would have been difficult to have carried out such work in a violent or even sporadically hostile environment, even with a miltary screen, for it would have pinned down hundreds of troops for weeks on end. But again, it is probably a mistake to under-estimate Roman determination and techniques.

Incidentally, Ivan Margary, who in his classic description of the Roman roads system of Britain accorded the Peddars Way the designation 33b, also computed the distance from Ixworth to Holme as a fraction over 48 miles. This would not have been how the Romans saw it, of course, as their measurements were different.

The word 'mile' comes from the Latin milia passuum, which was roughly one thousand strides of about 5ft, making the Roman mile about 1611 yards (according to Raymond Chevallier; or 1480 metres) or some 150 yards shorter than today's standard distance. This would have put the measurement from Stanton Chare to Holme at about 51 Roman miles.

Chapter Three

Making connections

IF AS as seems likely the Peddars Way and the Fen Road (or Fen Causeway) both date from the Claudian/Neronian period, which means they were built a few years before or just after the Boudican revolt, then it is equally likely they are among the earliest of the Roman roads in the county. The Pye Road (The Magpie inn at Stonham is said to have had a magpie in a cage beside the road) doubtless sprang into being as a response to the subsequent growth of the township and administrative centre of Venta Icenorum, which was deliberately placed on a greenfield site close by another of the former Iceni tribal centres and even closer to river connections to the sea. The Pye, of course, was the first proper main road leading from Norfolk's new capital to Colchester and beyond, including London, and it ran west of the Roman town and was linked to the west gate by a bridge over the river Tas.

Many of Norfolk's known Roman roads survive today only as straight or disconnected stretches of lane, bits of track, hedge lines, green lanes, crop marks, or even as field or parish boundaries. But what is known is that a continuation of the Fen Causeway east-west road took a fork to the north-east and continued on from Denver through Crimplesham, Stradsett, Fincham (where it is known as the Fincham Drove, finally crossing the Way near Castle Acre), Kempstone, Billingford, Brampton, and perhaps beyond Wayford Bridge to the Isle of Flegg and Caister on Sea. Another important east-west line of communication, and another branch of the Fen road, took a much straighter course from Denver to Venta Icenorum (Caistor St Edmund) across the sandy wastes of Breckland and on through Threxton, Watton High Street, Scoulton, and thence to Crownthorpe and Ketteringham.

Yet another striking road (striking, because of a straight-edged plantation boundary which actually shows up on LandSat satellite colour enhanced images of the area) once linked the Roman settlement at Toftrees, near Fakenham, with the North Sea coast near Holkham close by the old Iron Age earthworks. Like the Peddars Way it, too, has no obvious coastal termination and seems to serve no obvious purpose save possible seabourne facilities. At what is now Haggard's Lodge it was crossed at 90 degrees by another road, possibly a single alignment patrol road, from Egmere to Barwick. Meanwhile, a 1906 excavation (Laver) at a Grimston villa site produced evidence suggesting that a Roman road ran from the village 'in a direct line as far as the Peddars Way,' which meant it would also have crossed a strand of the Icknield Way. Alas, no trace of this road appears to remain.

It is thus possible to surmise that the Peddars Way, the Pye, and the two east-west roads, formed the framework of a large and presumably continuously changing network of Romano-British roads, tracks and paths serving local and regional needs.

In addition to Venta, which came to stand at the centre of an increasingly important web of connecting roads as the area's focus shifted east from the Brecks, upwards of a dozen small towns, roadside settlements and large villages came into being, thanks to commercial impetus or the organic coming together of clusters of farms and home-steads.

So in a busy agricultural and industrial landscape one might expect that the Norfolk countryside was criss-crossed with lines of communications including roads for wagons and travellers, links between villages and settlements, tracks leading to farms, and even paths wandering to houses.

In one sense the Peddars Way fits somewhat self-conciously into this general pattern since its actual purpose and destination are still unknown. But it does not seem to have been one of the major bones of the later highway skeleton, though it is generally assumed it did link indirectly, if not directly, with Colchester. Indeed, it would be a very strange thing if it had not.

Margary, for example, was of the opinion it linked at Stanton Chare (a villa site; the Old English 'cerr' or 'cyrr' is thought to have meant 'turn') and Ixworth with the Long Melford and Pakenham road which, at its north-east extremity seems to die away in South Norfolk but which may have continued on to Crownthorpe and thus, by turning right, to Caistor St Edmund. Indeed, some maps of the network seem to emphasise this. But it is now more often than not linked at Stanton with the Stone Street and Bildeston road, thus giving a somewhat straighter link with Colchester. Indications of a continuation of this route south from Ixworth towards Colchester add weight to the feeling. Which ever is true, the junction at Stanton Chare was profoundly important. Left, and the traveller heading northwards went along the Peddars Way towards Holme and the sea. Right, and most probably it was to East Harling, Attleborough, Morley and Crownthorpe.

Did the Way offer a link with Colchester? Although not a continuous or single route, the answer is probably 'yes.' Ivan Margary clearly saw the Way as a branch road, even though it may have been more important than the road from which it sprang. Describing its 'robust form of construction,' he said the Peddars Way 'must not only have been constructed at a different date from the southern part of the road out of which it forks, but must also have been built upon more typically Roman principles and in weightier style.'

But wait. This may be misleading. Subsequent studies suggest the 'weightier style,' compared to roads in the south-east, may have been more to do with different soil conditions and therefore different construction methods, rather than specific purpose. For example, the Long Melford and Chelmsford road passes over sand and gravel, the Bildeston (Colchester) road over boulder clay. However, if the Way does eventually turn out to have been a branch road, or merely a spur leading north-west from Stanton Chare, the perhaps it was because the highway leading to Ixworth actually dates from

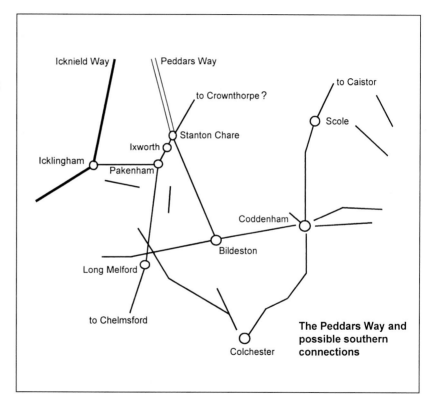

The Peddars Way and possible southern connections

the AD43/47 period (the Icknield Way and the old pre-Roman Peddars Way track satisfying needs at that point), while the slick, improved Way was hurried through post-AD61.

This is conjecture, however. But a link with Colchester - with its military significance - and Holme, at the mouth of the Wash, the Metaris Aest (where a fuzz of road possibilities and links make the Way's actual ending very problematical indeed), does seem logical.

It is important to emphasise that these matters are uncertain, for without actual dates and an actual construction sequence it is difficult to piece together the evidence with any sort of conviction. But in the end, what the Romans developed was a road network subsequently subject to over 300 years of changes of use, to abandonment, development and modification, to local tinkering, to the lives and deaths of industries, the fads of fashion and the needs of transportation. It would not have stayed still for very long. Just think, for example, how our road network has altered in the last 300 years.

Forward planning

Precisely how long the post-rebellion period of military revenge and bloody retribution lasted is not known, but it may have been many months in which case, with the harvest lost and the fields unsown, starvation surely stalked a landscape already scarred and pockmarked by destroyed villages, deserted animal paddocks and dead or scattered tribespeople.

It is temping to think that Paulinus, a canny operator at the best of times, gave the job of cleaning out this nest of native vipers to the battle-hardened 9th Legion, traditionally based at Longthorpe. The greater part of this legion had taken part of the victorious Anglesey campaign and had then marched with the main body of the army to Mancetter, where it had played an equally important role in the defeat of Boudica. But elements of the 9th, including its cavalry, had also been ambushed and destroyed by Boudica early in the campaign, when it rushed to intercept the rebels, and revenge would have been high on its list of priorities. So the 9th, backed by auxiliaries and others, would have had a considerable score to settle with the Iceni, and if Paulinus did indeed let them off the leash then there can be no doubt they did whatever had to be done with relish and considerable energy.

Some writers say the immediate after-effects of the rebellion, from an Iceni perspective, were at least two-fold. Almost a complete generation of old men, young men of marriageable age, and those women who might have attempted to emulate Boudica, were wiped out. Poverty, starvation and slavery must have further reduced the ranks of the few survivors. Both suppositions lead one to believe that the native population could not possibly have been restored to its original levels even in the space of a generation; and indeed, it is likely it never was.

But someone had to begin the forward planning. A future had to be mapped out. Because of the ferocious effectiveness of the military response it must also have been apparent to the Roman civil administration that the Iceni were finished as a fighting force (no permanent military occupation seems to have been imposed) and even as an identifiable entity, and that Rome therefore had yet another province on its hands.

Some stretches of road vital to military requirements may already have been in existence at this time, particularly if some construction operations had begun immediately after the revolt of AD47. But it is possible that at about this time, AD62 or AD63, thoughts were also being directed towards the looming question of how the territory was to be policed and governed, and therefore, if a larger network of connecting roads would be needed.

Right: The Way crosses the River Nar at Castle Acre

Perhaps the shape of a new political and economic landscape began to emerge through the smoke as the weeks and months passed, as retribution slowly turned into policing, and as pacification slowly evolved into Romanization. An expanded highways system may thus have been a priority on every official wish list, but even this does not entirely explain why the military authorities ordered the arduous and costly construction of the road which eventually came to be called the Peddars Way.

The ferry theory

Over the years there have been, by and large, three schools of thought relating to the question as to why the Peddars Way was actually built. The first was the troop movement theory, which holds that the road was built to aid policing, and more importantly and specifically, to facilitate the movement of troops travelling to and from Lincolnshire or even York or the Midlands, a necessary string to the Roman bow particularly early in the campaigns should these territories also have risen in revolt. A crossing of the Wash, it said, would help avoid a lengthy and unpleasant march through the misty, mired, waterlogged Fens on Nero's Fen Causeway. With such a scheme in place reinforcements could be rushed into or out of Iceni territory very quickly.

Which indeed they could.

The second was the intimidation theory. This suggested the road was constructed quite deliberately to pass through the tribal heartland of the Iceni, not only to enable troops to penetrate the area quickly and effectively but also to impress and physically intimidate the local tribal structure. The Way, it was thought, was an illustration of the might of Rome writ large upon the landscape.

The third school of thought was much more tenuous, a single skein drawn from the totality of the first theory. The Peddars Way, it said, was built because the Romans ran ferries over the Wash, initially for troops. What is more, these Norfolk-bound troop vessels were guided into a safe haven by a beacon built on a prominent place near Thornham. Thus the Way ran to some sort of wharf or landing place close to Holme or Thornham, perhaps in a tidal inlet long since lost to the encroaching sea. There may even have been a Roman land-settlement scheme for retired soldiers established in the vicinity of Holme, which certainly still looks possible.

The Thornham beacon theory was derived from an honourable background. The actual site is about 2.5km to the east of the Peddars Way and just over a mile from Thornham, which has a natural harbour. Immediately to the south of the site is a grassy track known as Greenbank, thought to be of great antiquity and which may even have come into being during the Iron Age. Further weight is added to the idea that this was the site of a beacon by Faden's map (1797), which marks it as Beacon Hill, and Bryant's map (1826), which calls the area Beacon Hill Wood. None of this, of course, rules out the possibility that the location may have been used as a beacon in later, post-Roman eras. Early excavations on the site were largely inconclusive in an interpretative sense, but in 1957 Rainbird Clarke, the eminent Norfolk archaeologist, in a lecture to the Society of Antiquaries, identified an extensive area of chalk pieces as a large foundation. He speculated that chalk dug from a massive nearby ditch may well have been used to construct a signal tower, or navigation mark, of gleaming white chalk placed upon the foundation. He also discussed the possibility that in Roman times a ferry linked the end of the Peddars Way at Holme with a Roman road running from Lincoln to Burgh le Marsh. The Thornham tower, or beacon, would thus have served as a sailing mark for Norfolk-bound ferries.

In 1975 CH Lewton-Brain, writing in the EDP, saw the site

Right: The Castle Acre to Massingham road snakes towards Shepherd's Bush

as the location of a Roman signal station perhaps associated with the later Brancaster Shore Fort. During one dig, he wrote, he and others found a ditch, some Roman pottery and a metal spoon, but no foundations. The excavators also turned up an Anglo-Saxon bead, and later, a bronze vessel handle and an Anglo-Saxon skeleton. So the site had at least been used from the Iron Age through to the Anglo-Saxon period. Some time later, and as a result of further excavation, thoughts about the chalk 'foundation' were modified, the Roman beacon idea being largely overtaken by fresh evidence.

The Thornham site now looks was though it was one of a group of nine distinctive enclosures identified in the northern half of the county, though the actual dating and function of them is still largely unknown. All seem to occupy relatively elevated ground with views over river valleys or the sea, but they were probably not purely defensive or offensive. Only three (Thornham, Warham Burrows, Wighton) have been excavated to any extent, and only Thornham has been tentatively dated. Iron Age finds have been relatively common in the area.

Thornham is a rectangular enclosure, like the others, massively ditched and with a single entrance. It was built on the site of earlier occupation. But was it a defended enclosure? Was it a storage depot? No-one is certain. What can be said is that the ditch and its ramparts seem alien to Roman military design practices, and they have therefore been marked down as the product of native planning. Nowadays the site is generally thought to post-date AD43, while it is presently unthinkable that it might have been built by the Iceni immediately after the Boudican revolt. So the construction of the Thornham enclosure, and its main period of use, is attributed to that narrow period of time between AD43 and AD61.

To sum up, the troop movement idea has always seemed somewhat flimsy for a number of reasons. It is surely unlikely that military commanders would have wanted to risk crucial troop movements, on a regular basis, on the twin vagaries of weather and sea conditions. Again, where would these troops have come from, or where would they have been going to? The Saxon Shore fort at Brancaster was centuries away, remember. So, Lincoln? Longthorpe? York? Colchester? A glance at a map of the Roman road system of Britain, I would have thought, also seems to rule out a Wash crossing as a best option. It would surely have been quicker to use the Fen Causeway, which may have been in place before the Boudican revolt.

As for the Thornham site, it looks as though it was an Iron

Age construction. No trace of a Roman beacon has ever come to light at this location. And while there may well have been a long lost wharf or landing place at the termination of the Peddars Way, I have to say that of the three explanations as to why the road was built, the intimidation theory still looks the best. But there is still something missing. There must have been other good reasons, too.

Summing up

There is no doubt that the Roman Peddars Way, as it was originally conceived, ran like a knife through the heartland of the Iron Age Iceni tribal landscape, and the suggestion that the road may have been built, in part, to impress and intimidate the natives is a compelling one. A parallel, perhaps, was the extraordinary tower-like structure at Stonea - with the nearby Stonea military camp - from which the Romans ran the Imperial Estate of the fens. These creations were very visible, political statements, imposed on former native territories. But the Way clearly had a practical importance, too, for a newly built road, drained and metalled and with most of the corners and deviations ironed out, would have had a considerable advantage over earlier boggy, wandering and inadequate tracks, the Icknield Way included.

It also seems clear the Way had some sort of affinity with the sea and presumably with some coastal destination now lost beneath the waves. At least one other Roman road in Norfolk - the Holkham road - also seems to possess this seaward motivation, while some say there is a suggestion of a third, similar road running roughly north or north-east from Brampton possibly in the general direction of Cromer. The first two, the Way and the Holkham road, today lead to flat, shallow beaches or salt marshes, while a Brampton-Cromer road, today at least, would terminate on top of cliffs. Of course, that may not have been the case 2000 years ago.

The intimidation theory, also touched on in the previous section, begs other questions, too, in that the time it could have taken to build the Way might have been longer than the actual period of military retribution and mopping-up operations which followed the Boudican revolt. In other words, if post-AD61 intimidation and troop movements were the only reasons for building the Peddars Way then it might have been largely obsolete before it was completed. Roman planners were not usually as short-sighted as this. Therefore, and leaving aside any question of ferries, it does seem that one of the major influences contributing to the puzzle is the sea, or rather, those miles of flat, shelving beaches, inlets, and salt marshes which predominate in most parts of the Wash and along the Norfolk coastline as far east as Weybourne.

During walking excursions along the Way my natural inclination was to walk towards the coast and the sea. Purely out of interest, however, I suggest you hold a map of Norfolk's Roman roads upside down. Now the Way and the Holkham road look suspiciously like highways leading inland rather than inland roads leading to the coast. Of course, it is necessary to keep in mind that present maps of the road system are almost certainly incomplete and therefore probably misleading.

There is plenty of evidence for early seaborne traditions. When the Rhine estuary flowed into the North Sea between Denmark and Yorkshire, Mesolithic travellers had access to areas which today are covered by the sea, and a number of barbed points have been found. At Tybrind Vig in Denmark skilled carpenters produced log boats complete with decorated paddles, while another Mesolithic log boat was discovered at St Albans some years ago. Closer home a wooden object, a handle and half a blade, was found in gravel workings at Bawburgh in 1987. Over 55in long and made of oak, it was subsequently dated to the Late Iron Age or possibly the Roman period, and while its function is uncertain it may well have been a steering oar. There is also a tradition that boats may have been used to transport Norfolk flint artefacts, and later, iron ore and gold objects, while it is known that even after the Roman period several of the county's rivers were navigable for shipping for considerable distances inland. There is also evidence on both sides of the Channel of trade with the Continent.

On a slightly different tack Raymond Selkirk (see Reading and References) believes that most Roman roads in the UK, which by and large avoid detours and continue on regardless, must have been generally unsuitable for large waggons and heavy haulage. The use of large waggons, he thinks, was restricted to roads close to towns, most long distance transport being by water. In other words, by sea and along inland streams and rivers.

It is known that the Roman army did have a long association with the sea and even a direct influence in naval affairs, which is not as surprising as it seems because land-sea operations were regularly carried out. The 2nd and 6th Legions, according to one reference, are even said to have recruited from the ranks of merchant seamen to the extent that their altar insignia included a sea creature curled round a staff, or trident. Another insignia included an anchor, and a fish-tailed goat. As for the 9th Hispania and its regional governor, Aulus Plautius, it is possible both were selected for the invasion force because of specialist knowledge they had gained in operations on the Danube. Thus the 9th's subsequent advance to the Thames and then northwards up the east coast may well have been supplied by the Classis Britannica, Rome's British fleet based at Boulogne, and later Dover.

The Roman navy was organised into at least nine separate fleets, the Classis Britannica having responsibility for the North Sea, the Channel and the Irish Sea. At least one of its ships is actually known, a bireme (which might have had up to 230 rowers) named Sabrina (the Latin name for the River Severn). As I was writing this book it was also being reported in a national newspaper that the remains of what was believed to be a Roman troopship had been located in the mud of the Tyne estuary. The empire could also call upon a large merchant fleet, of course.

But what of the Iceni? Even if they were not themselves involved in matters maritime (perhaps they preferred to be middlemen or agents rather than boat-builders or sailors), then at least they must have been familiar with the trade, for it seems reasonable to suspect that the Wash, despite its

Right: A former Ordnance Survey triangulation post still stands sentinal at Shepherd's Bush

mists, sandbanks, vicious tides and storms, was an anchorage or shipping landing area. Indeed, it would not overstretch the boundaries of possibility to suggest that the Iceni, who prior to AD61 had authority over miles of coastline and inland routes, may have been involved at some level or other with the sea trade, either as suppliers or traders, hauliers or chandlers. Again, perhaps there were wharves and harbours in the vicinity, now lost and covered by the sea. Maybe Roman traders beached their vessels hereabouts in pre-invasion days. Maybe ships carrying military reinforcements and supplies rode at anchor here. CH Lewton-Brain certainly believed in the existence of an early small port somewhere between Old Hunstanton and Holme, giving as evidence an extract from the Calendar Close Rolls of Edward 1, dated April 15, 1297, which evidently mention 'Nicholas de Holm and Robert de la Roche, keepers of the port of Holm and Hunstanton,' and list a vessel known as a cog and a cargo from Flanders, which presupposes a relatively large ship and a port of sufficient depth to accommodate it.

Admittedly, much of this is tenuous, but it does help to shift the narrow focus of the ferry theory into a wider one of a busy maritime coast, anchorages, beaches on which to beach vessels, and the prospect of wharves and landing areas among the sandbars and creeks of North West Norfolk. It is also, I confess, unsupportable on present evidence, though there are some conclusions which can be drawn with a degree of confidence.

For example, the Peddars Way really does run through the heart of the Iceni's Late Iron Age territory. Parts of the Way do look as though they might have been built either by the Roman military themselves or by civilian workers working to military specifications. And there is at least a degree of probability that Roman military men were in the area, in force and with serious intent, only after AD47 (following the first Iceni uprising) and for a few years immediately after the Boudican rebellion, possibly up to circa AD65. At least, there is no evidence of army operations in Norfolk beyond the end of this decade. Within this context the positioning of the Claudian fort at Threxton/Saham Toney must also be taken into account, along with the altered siting of the larger Neronian cavalry fort, the building of which caused the line of the Way at its crossing of Watton Brook to be modified.

Collecting all these matters together, it does seem there may have been a general tendency in the past to underestimate the importance of waterborne traffic. It also seems certain that if, for some reason, Roman troops did wish to cross the Wash then suitable vessels could have been found for them. But the word 'ferry' implies something more routinely ordered, perhaps even a time-tabled service, which seems unlikely. Generally, it is much more likely that the Wash embraced shipping of all descriptions associated with the comings and goings of traders, official passengers, and military men and supplies.

With all this in mind I would like to suggest that:

1. A pre-Roman track, in part possibly a strand of the Icknield Way, may have run through Brettenham and Threxton/Saham Toney, and possibly through parts of North West Norfolk. If so, it may have been used for commerce, including maritime trade.

2. Evidence suggests that the Roman military road now called the Peddars Way was constructed during a narrow 20-year period between AD43, the year of the Claudian invasion, and circa AD63. The three main suggestions are that it might have been built (a) circa AD44 as part of the Claudian advance; (b) circa AD47, in response to the first Iceni uprising; or (c) immediately after the Boudican rebellion, perhaps between AD61 and 63.

3. The present archaeological advice is that the road is probably Claudian rather than Neronian, which narrows the focus to between AD44 and AD54 and helps to make circa

AD47 look the most credible possibility. This was just after the first revolt was crushed and when pro-Roman factions of the Iceni seem to have gained political control. It is just possible that as part of a deal with Scapula they took on responsibility for the security and movement of Roman supplies from the coast. It should be noted, of course, that if the road was not actually already in being before the Boudican revolt, then there would have been an urgent need for it after, when security and agreements would have fallen apart and when army supply routes might still have been under threat from surviving dissidents.

4. Whatever the actual year of construction, the Way was built to facilitate the deployment of troops, assist patrols, and ensure the integrity of an important coastal connection; in other words, to provide a fast, protected route inland from North West Norfolk's anchorages and landing places.

Small town landscape

The gradual development of small towns and settlements in Norfolk during the Roman period is thought to have differed from the areas of the civitas capitals, which reached their peak in earlier centuries. One illustration of this is that Venta's defensive walls, built in the 3rd century AD, surrounded an area much smaller than the original township. Aerial photographs also show networks of roads away from the central core. It all suggests there was a contraction of the capital before the walls were actually built.

One possible explanation is high inflation. Because of this evident financial difficulty, tributes (the taxes imposed by the authorities) may have been collected in kind rather than in cash, leaving the smaller towns and settlements much better placed to deal with the prevailing conditions. At the very least, Norfolk's smaller settlements seem to have reached their peak in the 3rd and 4th centuries AD, growing in stature and size alongside an increasing range of agricultural and industrial activities.

The actual location of Venta Icenorum, at Caistor St Edmund, may have been chosen not only because the area had once been a focus of Neolithic and Iron Age settlement and that it was, in effect, a green-field site, but also because of certain geographical advantages. For example, it was just off the edge of the difficult clay soils, transport and communication routes were good, and it was beside the River Tas. This was to become increasingly important, for it allowed for riverine transport - probably shallow wooden boats similar to the Norfolk keel - to and from the local coastal ports.

Water transport must have been a key factor, for road transport, except for purely local purposes, was thought to have been slow, clumsy and expensive. According to one calculation it was about 25 times more expensive than transport by water. The problem was that horses and oxen hauling heavy waggons, even over the best of roads, could not cope with any great weight. The total burden of the load therefore had to be limited, and a speed of about two to three miles an hour was probably routine. Another problem was that eight oxen ate more weight in fodder than they could actually pull in a day, so unless each load was of very

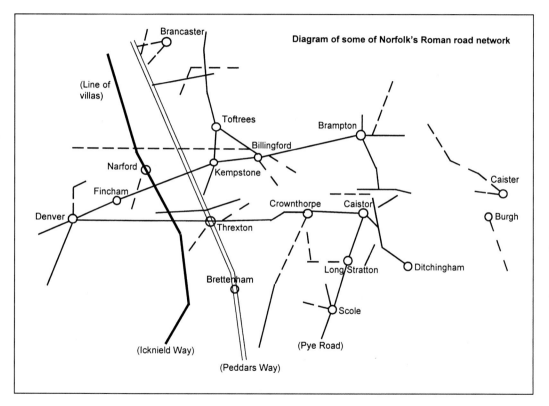

Diagram of some of Norfolk's Roman road network

Brancaster
(Line of villas)
Toftrees
Billingford
Brampton
Narford
Kempstone
Caister
Fincham
Crownthorpe
Caistor
Denver
Threxton
Burgh
Long Stratton
Ditchingham
Brettenham
Scole
(Icknield Way)
(Pye Road)
(Peddars Way)

The road framework in Roman Norfolk in the centuries following the Boudican revolt seems to have centered on Caistor St Edmund, and to have incorporated at least two west to east corridors of travel high value then road transport over a considerable distance was clearly uneconomic. Not until the Middle Ages did large-scale long distance land transport become a realistic proposition.

In Norfolk, the locations of fewer than 20 small to large Romano-British settlements have been identified, but there is an element of logic about them. They give the impression of being strung out relatively evenly along the road network, at road junctions and/or river crossings, and at approximately 10 to 15km intervals. These sites include Hockwold, Denver, Fincham, Narford, Kempstone, Wicklewood/Crownthorpe, Toftrees, Billingford, Dunton, Walsingham/Wighton, Scole, Needham, Long Stratton, Ditchingham, Brampton, and two along the Peddars Way, Brettenham and Saham Toney/Threxton.

Only three have been examined in any detail, but most seem to have grown as ribbon development along the road frontages and to have had other roads or lanes added for access to properties. Many of these lanes do not seem to echo deliberate planning decisions, but reinforce the impression that they may have arisen because of natural inclincation and local convenience. Nevertheless, recent work at the University of East Anglia (EDP, July 28, 2001) suggests that an element of landscape planning may have been employed.

Brampton alone had defences, which protected a central core area of about like 15 acres, while Scole and Billingford seem to have marked the limits of their settlement areas with ditches. Most of them probably developed before the end of the 1st century AD, though early Roman military forts at Saham Toney/Threxton, Billingford and Scole may have influenced the growth of these particular towns. It is certainly possible that others developed from the earlier establishment of staging posts.

Temple sites have been identified at Walsingham/Wighton, Wicklewood/Crownthorpe and Scole, but at some other locations a ritual/religious element does not appear to have been a particularly important factor. Figurines depicting Mercury have been found at Great Walsingham, Crownthorpe, Brampton, Tuttington and at the Caister on Sea fort and vicus, a small associated settlement. Venus figurines have been discovered at Burgh Castle and Tharston, while there is evidence from Elsing and Thetford, in Central and South Norfolk, of the worship of Pan. In addition, dedications to the native god Faunus (a woodland deity also associated with the Roman god Pan) are known from inscriptions among the Thetford Treasure.

By and large the territory on both sides of the Peddars Way, and elsewhere, remained essentially rural in character, a countryside of settlement groups and farmsteads. For reasons not fully understood, however, very few of these small towns retained any degree of local importance or influence much beyond the 5th century AD.

Country life

Over in the far west of the former Iceni territory, and during the 1st century AD, a gradual reduction in sea levels meant that large tracts of hitherto uninhabitable and unusable fen land slowly dried out and became available. Because it was 'new' land, and had no previous owner, it automatically became the property of the emperor. In time, these new lands were to be managed and administered as a large Imperial Estate run by officials centered on a head-quarters at Stonea in Cambridgeshire, the focus of their enterprise being sheep rearing (for their milk, wool and hides) and salt production. Excavation suggests the estate labourers probably led a somewhat muted, basic, and even downright miserable life, so perhaps most of the profits were shipped out elsewhere.

Some 200 years later, and beyond the patchwork of the small towns and villages of the developing Romano-British

Right: The Way on Massingham heath

landscape, a new style of living was also beginning to emerge, for influencial members of society began to build comfortable country residences. The sites of about twenty such buildings are known in Norfolk, most of them constructed from chalk, flint and local carstone, or perhaps Barnack stone brought in through the fens. An impressive line of these villas once graced the route of the old Icknield Way in North West Norfolk, on the seaward side of the Peddars Way where the two ancient lines of communication came into particularly close proximity.

For much of its length Norfolk's stretch of the Icknield Way seems to have been an ill-defined network of tracks or droveways running, in North West Norfolk, along the higher ground just above the spring line. A slightly higher and presumably somewhat drier route seems to have been favoured in winter, while another branch which ran closer to the spring line may have been the summer route. These springs may well have made the location attractive to the developers, who were presumably prosperous officials, farmers and landowners. On the other hand this corner of North West Norfolk, for some reason, had always been different and important, so there may have been kudos to be derived from actually living there.

Ten villas are known to have existed close to the Icknield Way (Gayton Thorpe, Gayton, Grimston, Congham, Flitcham, West Newton, Appleton, Heacham, and two at Snettisham), some of them quite luxurious and utterly unlike anything the natives would have seen before, except possibly in Romanized towns. They were large, well appointed farmhouses, some with mosaics, decorated plaster walls and hypocausts, and they demonstrate deliberate and fashionable aspirations towards a distinct Roman life-style.

Dating evidence suggests an appetite for this sort of lifestyle in this area in the 3rd and 4th centuries AD, and it is assumed their economies - for they seem to have been run like country estates - were based largely on agriculture, possibly the provision of livestock for slaughter. Interestingly, none of these villa sites are close to a known major town, so it is possible the focus of their trade was either Narford or Brancaster. Indeed, Brancaster or its allied settlement may have been some sort of a collection point or even a shipment centre for state supplies of salted meat and perhaps leather.

It is certainly possible that roads and lanes connected the villas with the Peddars Way, and there may have been a connecting link between the Way and Brancaster. History also suggests that if the monied classes living on these estates called for improvements to the nearby roads and byways, as they surely did, then they would no doubt have got them.

Much earlier, and probably from the late Iron Age onwards, smelting was also carried out in the area, along with a certain amount of salt-making, an industry which was to prosper in North West and West Norfolk during the Norman period, too. In addition, there were large potteries at Brampton, while in West Norfolk, by the 2nd century, the pottery kilns had tended to become concentrated in the Nar valley area, from where they may eventually have won a military contract. Around AD250, when the 1st Aquitain cavalry occupied the new fort at Brancaster, Nar Valley ware was used extensively. By about AD350, however, the Nar Valley industry had all but disappeared. Incidentally, the fort at Brancaster probably pre-dates any serious Saxon threat so, with Caister on Sea and Reculver (Kent) - the earliest Saxon Shore forts - it could possibly be more about controlling trade and protecting shipping.

Clearly, there was a considerable amount of agricultural and industrial activity taking place on both sides of the Peddars Way, and particularly round the Icknield Way and in the Nar valley, all of which makes the apparent absence of a large neighbourhood town even more surprising. It may simply be the case that such a town has not been identified. If so, then Narford may indeed be an obvious candidate. Located close to where the Icknield Way crosses the Nar and where an Iron Age fort once controlled the crossing, there is evidence of native and Roman activity. A series of coins, the dates of which continue to AD400, also hints there may have been something more than a large villa here. Whether or not Narford was a local market centre is a question to be answered in the future. If it does turn out to be the case, then it is possible that a shift in the focus of traffic had taken place and that Narford was one of the factors which contributed to the post-Boudican decline of the Peddars Way.

Meanwhile, just over the border in Suffolk, but still on the line of the Peddars Way, something similar was taking place at Stanton Chare where excavation unearthed an unusually elaborate example of a Roman farm and estate. The digs, in 1935/36, dated a series of wooden buildings to years prior to AD130 and also uncovered the fact that they had been subsequently converted and extended. There were several other buildings, too, the functions of which were not fully understood. There was a room with a hypocaust, an aisled building with internal painted plaster, gravel paths and a bath house, but the site, which evidently lasted until at least the end of the 4th century, was large and confused. Sections excavated just before the Second World War may have represented merely the wing of an even larger complex.

An end in sight

The geographical spread of the Roman empire was immense, too large, in any event, to police with the number of legions then in existence. So the rulers sought another method of enslavement, another means of control. Instead of tightening the screw on native populations in an attempt to keep them cowed and resentful, they relaxed the restrictions. Instead of persecution they encouraged Roman culture and then shared with them the evident benefits of the new arrangement. Some of the natives grew contented and rich.

In this, the highways played their part. Once the main structure of the road network had been built, and once its advantages became apparent, many previously isolated communities slowly began to forge a sort of attachment to the passing travellers and thus to the passing trade. Fashionable foreign goods flooded in, too, trailing in their wake new aspirations and a new way of life, in much the way

Right: Chalk outcrop visible near Harpley

Americanisation has more recently conquered the West. Anyway, the old tribal system was broken beyond repair, so the island simply began to re-invent itself. Maybe it is at this point that we can perceive the beginnings of a nation. A series of excavations at Scole in the 1990s helped to paint a picture of life on and around Norfolk's Roman roads. Scole evidently developed from a crossroads site on the Roman road leading from Colchester to Caistor St Edmund, where it crossed the River Waveney, and an east-west road which may have led towards Brettenham. One reason for Scole's apparent staying power may have been its distance from the capital, for it probably flourished as a local market town.

The east-west road was found to date to the late 1st century AD, and interestingly, it was only partially metalled. Perhaps construction costs dictated that metalling was confined to the centre part of town. In the vicinity of the metalling, however, there were a number of individual plots with boundaries and stakes, and some areas contained timber buildings, a few of them end-on to the road. Some of these plots had wells. A range of activities took place either beside or in the vicinity of the road, including iron working and tanning, so this may have been the dirty, smelly edge of the town. The road, incidentally, was 12m wide, and somewhat unusually there was a gap between the edges of the metalling and the ditches. This may have been for flood protection rather than traditional drainage. There were also public facilities beside the road, including a square pit, a well, and what may have been washing facilities attached to a wayside loo. To the east of the road was a modest Romano-British temple.

Wayside facilities were not unusual in the Roman world. In 1990 the spring issue of the National Trust newsletter for East Anglia reported the discovery of the Roman equivalent of a motorway service station on the Wimpole Hall estate in Cambridgeshire. There, beside the Ermine Street road (London, Peterborough, York) archaeologists found a series of what they interpreted as horse paddocks, gardens and house plots. Horse bones were also uncovered, along with coins dating from AD250 to 300. It is believed the site could have been a posting station where messengers and travellers stopped, refreshed themselves and took on fresh horses.

After all, people travelled a surprising amount in the days of the empire, walking or riding on horseback or on a vehicle, of which there was a large range of types including light and open carts, two-wheeled covered gigs and many sorts of waggons. In the vicinity of the roads there were small towns and settlements, stalls selling goods, black-smiths, stables, horse dealers, temples, milestones and inns. The passers-by included military and official traffic, traders, merchandisers, criminals, sellers of produce, seamen between ships, muleteers, and so on.

But all things eventually come to an end, and the end of Roman rule in Britain is usually dated to about AD410, by which time Britain was being invaded from across the North Sea while at the same time the Roman army was being withdrawn to defend the empire from barbarian hordes from across the Danube. But that is only part of the end-game story. As early as the 3rd century tribes from across the sea were beginning to attack the eastern coastline of Britain, though the problem was probably much more widespread than that. In reality the whole of the northern frontier of the empire was being threatened, and as early as AD401 the withdrawal of troops was being actively considered. One definite Roman response was to develop and adopt the defensive system of the Saxon Shore, a joint army/navy operation. One legion (5000 men) was also sent home, but the chaos at the heart of the troubled empire worsened, and in AD406 the Rhine was crossed by German tribes who, within three years, reached the shores of the English Channel.

Evidence for the continued Roman occupation of Europe goes on for a long time, but in Britain it seems to have been a slightly different story. Many larger Roman buildings slowly disappeared, or were damaged, or had their struc-tures carted away. At the same time other evidence suggests the cut-off may not have been sudden or suddenly com-plete. For example, in AD429 St Germanus came to Britain to investigate a heresy, Pelagianism. His biographer noted afterwards that there had been Saxon incursions in the south, though elements of Roman life still continued and magistrates were still in charge in the cities. He also described Britain as 'a very wealthy island,' but of course he could have been referring to its potential. It is also known that by AD685, at Carlisle, the Roman buildings had been substantially rebuilt in timber, the roads were still being maintained, and the aqueduct was still in use.

To all intents and purposes, however, Roman jurisdiction was long gone. Only their influence and their ruined monuments remained.

Decline and change

It would seem the loss or banishment of Roman administra-tion and influences was not sudden, or even clearly defined, for despite the confusion and political manoeuvring of the time some elements of Romanization remained in place, or at least in fashion, for a considerable period. By the same token, and following the terminal decline of Venta Icenorum, no fully fledged town can be perceived in Norfolk before the 9th century, though it is possible some origins of urbanisation can be glimpsed at such places as Norwich and Thetford.

But new landmarks did begin to appear on the landscape - linear earthworks. Precisely who built them and why is still uncertain, but it is thought some of them relate to the 5th and 6th century period of political fragmentation. They may have been symbols of power and influence erected by long-forgotten princes, or perhaps attempts to regulate exchange and taxes at the boundaries of petty kingdoms. All that can be said is that the erection of them would have taken a great deal of time and required the mobilisation of many people.

One among them, known as the Launditch, east of Castle Acre near Longham, and long thought to be post-Roman, has now been re-assigned to an Iron Age date. Of the others, the Birchamditch (Narborough, running towards the Wissey) is also possibly Iron Age; the Fossditch (north-west of Thetford, between rivers Wissey and Little Ouse) is certainly post-Roman; while Panworth ditch (near Ashill) is possibly post-Roman. Then there is the Devil's Ditch, near East Harling. All are within ten miles of either side of the Peddars Way, but whether they had any relationship to it is another matter. They do seem to block or guard other Roman roads leading roughly west-east and crossing the Way on the higher ground.

By this time the Way may have been facing its second period of gradual decline, the first having occurred when the Roman army left the area after the Boudican rebellion had been put down and when the road's military usefulness evaporated. It may also have declined in importance as a line of communication once the central boulder claylands and the watershed to the east began to be opened up, thus allowing activities to become spread over a wider area. Further large-scale development also took place during the Norman period when, among other projects on or close to the Way, monastic houses were built at Thetford, West Acre and Castle Acre. This latter settlement was a Norman creation, being a planned town sited next to a castle built by William de Warenne. Construction of the castle and its great swathe of earthworks, which enclosed about seven acres, probably necessitated modification to the original Roman line of the Peddars Way. To the north of the settlement the line of the Way cannot really be detected again until the Massingham road is reached, while to the south the road is lost, on the surface at least, between Great Palgrave and Hungry Hill. Even so, and despite any possible decline in importance, the road clearly remained a venerable and noticeable mark on the landscape, for the boundaries of a number of Hundreds and even more parishes pay their respects to it.

The Hundred administrative unit evolved following the English re-conquest of the area from the Danes, for Domesday listed 33 such divisions in Norfolk, which means that by this time they were clearly well established. Indeed, they remained as sub-units of local government until as late as 1834. Some Hundreds seem to have used rivers or Roman roads as boundaries, while other Hundred meeting places were near fords, hills or mounds. Leets were small groups of settlements brought together for the purposes of geld collection, and they were also recorded in Domesday for Norfolk and Suffolk. Each Hundred composed a number of leets. There were 14 in South Greenhoe, for example. Wayland and South Greenhoe Hundreds both made use of the Way as an element of their boundaries, while a section of the Freebridge Hundred ran alongside it. Where the Way crosses a stream by a small bridge at Wretham - or Stone Brig, as it was still called in 1915 - was the place where the court for the Shropham Hundred was held, while at a site where the Way crosses the A11 there was in medieval times a stone cross which is said to have given its name to the Hundred of Guiltcross (formerly Gydecross). According to WG Clarke, the Suffolk Hundred of Blackbourn may have taken its name from the Blackwater ford, where the Way crosses the Little Ouse river.

Fring Cross, on the other hand, is thought to derive its name from the ancient crossroads. Between the 12th and 15th centuries the river meandering from Fring to Heacham, which today is more often than not a mere trickle, and sometimes disappears altogether, brought diverse benefits into the area. This modest waterway produced fish, provided irrigation, watercress, osier and hazel coppices, drove watermills, and it is also thought to have been used for the transportation of agricultural produce. Sedgeford, astride the Icknield Way and with the Peddars Way immediately to the east, was also handily placed.

Parish boundaries made even more use of the old road than the Hundreds did. They may date from the 9th or 10th centuries and some possibly related to economic rather than ecclesiastical needs, even though most parishes had at least one church. The smallest surviving unit of local administration some are, nevertheless, of great antiquity. Others may have appeared because of boundary changes or settlement disappearances. At least one set of parish boundaries emphasise the importance of water. At Rymer in Breckland, eleven of them converge on a cluster of small meres. Nearly half of Norfolk's stretch of the Way is parish boundary, something which underlines the road's unique position of importance in the landscape. In the north-west of the county, and prior to the circa 1920 parish reorganisation, Snettisham, Fring, Shernbourne, Great Bircham, Anmer, Dersingham, Flitcham cum Appleton and Harpley all used the Way to a greater or lesser degree. In Central Norfolk, Sporle with Palgrave and Swaffham did likewise, while closer to the Suffolk border Threxton, Merton, Tottington, Thompson, Stow Bedon, East Wretham, Breckles, Hockham, Illington, and Rushford and West Harling, ran alongside the road. The edges of the latter two boundaries were marked by stones, two of which were, the last time I walked this length, still visible in the undergrowth beside the Way a little way north of the Little Ouse ford at Knettishall. There may have been other similar marker stones, too.

Later, markets sprang up throughout the county, some alongside or near to the Way, including Saham Toney and Watton (established 1204), Merton (1227), Swaffham (1257), Little Massingham and Hockham (1272), Stanford (1283), Harpley (1302) and Fring (1372). There were also markets at Thetford and Castle Acre.

Deserted medieval sites also abound, and are a book in their own right. Along the line of the Peddars Way the sites of DMVs have been noted at West Harling (Thorpe Farm), close to the river Thet, and immediately east of the Way at Thorpe Street (where there may have been a watermill), Starkisey and Thursmore Street (Thrussemere). Yet more sites have been identified at Gasthorpe, Riddlesworth, Middle Harling, Roudham, Illington, Little Hockham, Threxton, Houghton on the Hill, Great and Little Palgrave, Gnatingdon and Houghton.

In the centuries following the Roman occupation the road also became acquainted with another sort of traveller - the pilgrim. Two of the most important centres in England were Canterbury (Kent) and Walsingham, where the original shrine stood for 500 years before it was destroyed in the 16th century. Norfolk also had a another centre for pilgrimage, Bromholm, near Bacton, but Walsingham was the most influential, at one time even rivalling Canterbury. Several kings and many notables made pilgrimages to Norfolk, and at one stage the 'waie from Walsingham to London' was said to have been one of the 20 most important thoroughfares in the country, while the Milky Way (said to point across the heavens to 'England's Nazareth') was known to the devout as the Walsingham Way. Pilgrims poured into Norfolk from many directions, and according to Leonard Whatmore one route from London took advantage of a section of the Peddars Way. This was the route which came through Tottenham and Ware to Newmarket, over Brandon ferry, through Weeting (by the cross at Mount Ephraim, where a section of the old medieval road still survives), Hilborough and North Pickenham. Here, the pilgrims crossed the Wissey, possibly using the section of the Way from Pickenham Wade to Procession (or Sessions) Lane, where they turned towards Litcham and Walsingham along another and now disappeared section of Roman road. On March 17, 1517, Charles Brandon, Duke of Suffolk, in a letter to Henry VIII, wrote that four days earlier, on Friday the 13th, he had met Queen Catherine of Aragon at 'Pykenham Wade' on her way to Walsingham, and had escorted her for the rest of the journey. If there was no bridge over the Wissey at the time then perhaps some wading had to be done.

Another important pilgrim route is thought to have been through West Acre and Flitcham, presumably crossing the Peddars Way somewhere on Massingham Heath north of Harpley Dams. But in addition to royalty and pious travellers, one senses the roads were also busy with the unemployed, misfits, ex-soldiers, beggars, the landless and the homeless, itinerants and 'roguish entertainers.'

The Way was still a significant line on the landscape in 1800 when Joseph Hill carried out a survey of the Houghton Hall estate.

He examined and made use of estate records going back to about 1600, and thus the Peddars Way appeared on a map of Thomas Rodwell's farm at Great Bircham and was also shown on the records of 1600. It appeared again on plans of Edmund Holland's farm (Great Bircham), Thomas Herring's farm (Harpley), Anthony Beck's farm (Great Massingham) and William Banks senior's farm (also Great Massingham), while on William Banks junior's farm at Great Massingham it is shown as having been crossed by the road from Litcham to King's Lynn, then the main central Norfolk route to the Wash. This road later fell into partial disuse.

Edmund Walker's farm (at Harpley) is of particular interest for here a map of 1720 recorded a curving track, also called the Peddars Way but clearly not the Roman road, which had for some reason been destroyed or removed by about 1800. It is useful evidence, first, that modification to the road and track system was being carried out, and second, that the word 'peddars' - of which there will be more in the next section - was associated with other roads and tracks.

Origins of the name

In 1990 the writer Iman Wilkens published a book called Where Troy Once Stood in which he argued that the events of the Iliad and the Odyssey, Homer's epic poems, occurred around the Channel and the Atlantic and that Troy, instead of being located in Turkey, was situated close to Cambridge near the Gog Magog Hills and Wandlebury Ring. Moreover, he wrote, The Wash was most likely the Thracian Sea, the river Yare was the Caystrius and the Thet the Thymbre, King's Lynn was Lyrnessus, and the hill of Samos was somewhere near present-day Sandringham. As for the Peddars Way, its name echoed that of Pedasos (a town sacked by Achilles) on the Satniois river (otherwise the Little Ouse). This was an interesting idea, but he offered little further evidence.

The fact remains that if the Romans did actually have a name for this particular stretch of road then we have no knowledge of it, or at least it has not been recognised. Nor

Right: This section of the Way is hardened as it approaches Harpley Dams

does the Way seem to have been recorded in the Tabula Peutingeriana (the Peutinger Table), which may have been compiled in the third century, or the Antonine Itineraries which, locally, tended to concentrate on London to Caistor St Edmund via Colchester and another London-Caistor route taking in Cambridge, Chelmsford and Scole. This evident omission may, of course, underline the later importance of administrative or even communication routes, or a decline into relative obscurity. But the effect is the same. The name Peddars Way is certainly not Roman. However, there is overwhelming evidence for the general form of this name relating to this particular road. CH Lewton Brain, for example, found the name Peddars Way on a Flitcham map of 1580, a Snettisham map of the 16th century, and on a 17th century Sedgeford map, which called it Street Way alias Peddars Way. In addition, Karl Inge Sandred of Uppsala University, who was studying Scandinavian place-names in Norfolk at the time, listed in a booklet sent to the author in 1979 - Peddersty, 1423; Pedderes Lane, 1425; Pedderesty, 1423-1462; Pedderysty, 1450s; Pedderstey, 1512; and Pedderstie, 1561. In the 1970s, at Norfolk Record Office, he also unearthed a 16th century map on which at least part of the old road was called Stretegate, possibly derived from the Old English

stig, meaning path, or Old Scandinavian, stigr, which had a similar meaning.

WG Clarke wrote that Faden's map of Norfolk (1797) named the road the Peddars Way. On another map of 1824 it was called Peddars Road, though the middle section was evidently often called Pedlar's Way. EM Beloe favoured Padder's Way, though I have never seen this spelling anywhere else. Anyway, padder might simply be a Norfolk mis-pronunciation and mis-spelling of pedder. White's Directory of 1845 merely added to add to the confusion by recording that the road was 'now called Pedler's Way.' The medieval English word pedder seems to have been a derivation of pedde, meaning pannier, or pedlar, one who carried goods. A ped was also a semi-circular wicker basket, used as a pannier for pack animals or as a carrier basket strapped on the back, usually to carry produce, or sometimes salt. Norwich market, I believe, once had a special area for ped sellers who displayed their fresh fruit and vegetables straight from the ped on to the dirt road surface. But the matter is more complicated than this for it is also clear that the name peddar, in its various forms, is not exclusive to our Roman road. There are other references to other paths sharing the name. For example: Le Pedderysty alias dicta Saltersty - possibly relating to a salters' road, from a document of 1585 dealing with the Icknield Way near Beachamwell; related by WG Clarke, In Breckland Wilds.

Peddars Lane - 1826, between Thurlton and Raveningham.

Peddars Way - 1720, but destroyed before 1800; a track near Edmund Walker's farm at Harpley.

Peddars Way - early manuscript maps of Fornham and Barnham, relating to a road which may have linked the Icknield Way with the main Peddars Way; recorded by Norman Scarfe in The Suffolk Landscape.

Peddars Way - southern edge of Christchurch Park, Suffolk.

Pedders Weye - 1587 map of Lessingham, relating to a road near the common leading to the church.

Peddars Way - maps of 1589 and 1718, relating to footpaths or sheepwalks on Mousehold Heath, Norwich.

Peddars Way - on a 1577 map of John Reve's land east of Cawston.

Peddars Way - on Faden's map, 1797, between Stockton and Haddiscoe.

Peddars Lane - one at Beccles; one at Fulmodeston, near Fakenham.

To add further to the general confusion, some parts of the road seem to have had their own presumably local name.

For example, WG Clarke said in 1914 that the southern part of the road's course in Norfolk, through the parishes of Hockham, Roudham, Brettenham and Bridgham, was often known as Ridgerow Road, Ridge Road or Ridgeway Road, a name which also appeared in an Enclosure Act document relating to Hockham. Between Wretham and Roudham Heath it was known as Deal Row, when (in 1913/14) it was a green trackway bordered by 'gnarled pines, crab apple trees and thickets of bramble - the most picturesque portion of its course.' The gnarled pines are still there, but I venture to suggest this section is no longer quite as attractive as it evidently was.

To sum up, the name Peddars Way is not Roman and clearly not exclusive to this one road. In Norfolk some sections also had different local names, some of which were still being used in the mid-20th century. The generic label Peddars Way (or its various forms) seems to have emerged during the Late Medieval to the 16th century period, the name generally indicating a track for foot traffic, for pedlars or people selling or carrying goods or produce, or droving animals, mainly sheep. It may be that the word pedder was once in general or widespread use and that over the centuries it gradually colesced into the one recognisable name on this one recognisible road.

Chapter Four

Evolution and change

LARGE tracts of the Norfolk landscape through which the old Roman road passes on its way to the sea are still dominated by agricultural and sporting estates which over the centuries altered the look of the countryside to a substantial degree. Among them are Merton, South Pickenham, Houghton, Sandringham and Holkham. On the light soil lands it was sheep rather than cattle which dominated the early livestock enterprises. One method evidently unique to Norfolk and parts of North West Suffolk was known as 'fold course,' whereby the manorial lord had the right to graze his sheep over his tenants' strips in the open fields after harvest and until sowing the following spring. He also had the right to graze his flocks on fallow land in the summer. The manure was of benefit to arable cropping, but the system also reinforced the not inconsiderable class divisions. By and large it forced tenants to rely on their arable crops for income. And of course, arable crops were not as lucrative as sheep.

In the late 18th century the best managed estate in Norfolk was that of the Cokes at Holkham, and it was Thomas William Coke, in 1776, who began to hold his annual sheep-shearings, which rapidly developed into important agricultural occasions. From about 1790 onwards agricultural improvements in Norfolk were dominated by Coke, and by Lord Townshend of Raynham, whose enthusiasm for farming earned him the nickname Turnip Townshend. Improved breeds and better crop rotation systems fuelled a revolution in the countryside, until by 1750 there were few strip fields left. And so, slowly, the 18th and early 19th centuries came to mark a period of great improvement which reached a climax in the 'high farming' enterprises of the mid-19th century. Alas, it was followed by an almost inevitable agricultural depression and a fall in grain production from the 1870s onwards.

Some idea of the pattern of landscape change, particularly along the line of the Peddars Way, can be gleaned by comparing Faden's map with that of Bryant. Even in the two or three decades squeezed between the Faden (1797) and Bryant (1826) maps, many greens, heaths and commons disappeared as agricultural modernising gained rapid momentum. Whether because of design considerations or because of simple statements of fact, Bryant, for example, does not show Anmer Common, Sporle Common, Coates Common, Necton Heath, Thompson Heath or Breccles Heath. However, the heaths of Harpley, Massingham and

Pickenham are still represented. If these omissions are an indication of the large-scale absorption of open land into the agricultural system then certainly by the early 1800s, if not well before, farming was pressing close on both sides of the old road.

In a sense the Way's importance as a north-west/south-east through route had gone. Instead, many of the local trade routes tended to be towards the ports of King's Lynn, Cley, Wells and Yarmouth. Thus obscurity beckoned for the Way, and thus, in some cases, stretches of the road became mere adjuncts to and even part of local farms. In other words, and in all but a few places, it settled into a new life as a useful and occasionally used farm track.

This emerging rural domesticity can also be seen in a number of other names gleaned once again from the Bryant map. For example, the 1826 Bryant marks the Way's present crossing of the A148 King's Lynn to Fakenham road as Harpley Wash, and it also marks nearby Harpley Dam House, underlining the importance of water for livestock.

The farming context is repeated west of the Way between Castle Acre and Old Wicken where a lane, or perhaps a building, is shown as Peddar Barn. Meanwhile, and switching to administration, today's detached section of the Way

immediately north of North Pickenham is labelled as Sessions Lane (now Procession Lane, derived from the beating of the bounds). However, Drunken Drove, north of Massingham Heath, defies interpretation unless it derives from one of Chesterton's English drunkards who helped inspire the rolling English roads.

Nevertheless, there is some slight indication that the old road might still have been used for middle distance live-stock droving. KJ Bonser included the line of the Peddars Way on a map of cattle droving routes through East Anglia to London, though to be honest it is hard to see quite how it might have been so utilised. Published in the early 1970s, Bonser's book describes the Way as 'for many miles an embanked green trackway along a chalk ridge,' adding that following the departure of the Romans it was used by pack-horses, smugglers and drovers.

There may be a touch of literary licence here for scarcely anywhere, at least nowadays, can the road be described as embanked. However, Bonser goes on to explain that after the drovers (presumably those engaged in the long-distance Scotland-Norfolk trade, or the local markets trade) had settled their accounts (receiving their dues, paying wages, settling grazing fees, and so on), which was evidently traditionally completed at inns such as the Angel at North

Walsham, they would proceed south using the ancient trackways.

The use of the Way for medium or long-distance cattle droving does not seem to me to make much sense for those herds turning turning off the main Scottish route into Norfolk (Wisbech, Setchey, Swaffham, St Faith's) at Swaffham in order to reach grazing grounds in the Waveney areas of Scole, Wortham, Botesdale, Hoxne, Harleston and even Walsham-le-Willows. There is more confidence in the notion that it may have been used for the movement of sheep.

Harley Common, Harpley Dams and Harpley Wash (Bryant, 1826) were sheep areas, as no doubt were some of the other great commons; while Faden (1797) indicated a ford and sheepwash close to the Way at Thompson in the Brecklands. Bryant also indicated a sheepwalk near North Pickenham, while there are at least two places (one between Castle Acre and the Massinghams, the other close to where the Way crosses the present A11) known now or earlier as Shepherd's Bush.

It is also likely - the road having for some time lapsed into the role of a quiet backwater - that it was used by local folk carrying produce, walking or riding to market, as a short cut between west-east lines of communication, and by farmers, horses and carts, shepherds, carriers, pedlars, smallholders, tramps and probably also by gypsies. They reached England at the beginning of the 16th century when they were known as Gypcians or Gipsons, because it was thought they came from Egypt.

Mention of pedlars reminds me that I have often mulled over the possibility there might have been a connection, however slight, between the road and the legend of the Pedlar of Swaffham. The church of Swaffham, a few miles from the Way, has some wonderful pedlar carvings, and the proximity of the two (the carvings, and the name of the road) is intriguing. A certain John Chapman (a chapman was a barter-man, or pedlar) did pay for repairs to the church's north aisle in 1454, and the pedlar (or chapman) may have used it on his professional travels or even travelled a stretch of it on his legendary journey to London, where he evidently went to find his fortune. (See: Other features along the Way).

Shortly before and just after the turn of the last century there was much confusion over the road's course and destination. According to WG Clarke, in 1872 it was referred to by one writer as the 'Roman road which leads from Brancaster to Swaffham,' while in 1904 it was said to link Brancaster, Castle Acre, Swaffham, Ickburgh,

Brandon, and thence Exning, Bishop's Stortford and Stratford-le-Bow. In 1908 yet another writer referred to it as a road which linked 'the two Branodunums, that to the south, now Brandon, and that to the north, now Brancaster.' All this must have come about through poor research, unreliable maps, confused writing or radical theories, for as Clarke also pointed out in 1914 the road had been more or less accurately described on Ordnance Survey maps, while only a year or two before he himself had walked the fifty miles 'of this most interesting primitive route,' returning with little doubt that it was correctly indicated. In passing, it would be interesting to know how Clarke did it. Did he camp overnight or stay at inns? How long did it take him? In might add that Faden and Bryant did a pretty good job describing its route, too.

But if agriculture brought about profound changes to the landscape beside and around the Peddars Way, then so in the 19th century did the advent of the railways lure more of the haulage and passenger business away from the old roads and tracks and on to the iron rails.

Inevitably, the Way did not remain aloof from these sweeping changes, and today bits and pieces of past and

Right: Bridle route logo and blackberries near Harpley, late October

present railway lines can still be seen along the road, for it was pierced by the metal rails at a number of places. For example, the Midland & Great Northern Joint Railway opened its Thetford to Norwich line in 1845. It crossed the Roman road at Roudham, not far from the old turnpike and the present A11 main road. Then in 1869 a railway company opened the Roudham Junction line to Swaffham, which also ran by Roudham beside the Way as far as Wretham. The main line is still used today on a daily basis but the branch line was closed in 1964. Even so, faint traces of its route can still be seen on the west side of the Way between Harling Drove and Wretham (Stonebridge), while old railway sleepers have been pressed into service for fencing purposes on the eastern boundary of the track. In addition, at Procession Lane just outside North Pickenham, the Roman road was crossed, by means of a bridge, by the M&GNJR Swaffham-East Dereham line (1848-1968), while a further spur crossed the Way near Sporle. The Great Eastern Railway's King's Lynn to Fakenham line (1879-1959) also once crossed the Way near Harpley Dams, while the M&GNJR Heacham to Wells line (1866-1952) passed over the Way just north of Sedgeford. Most of these new routes tended to confirm the dominance of modern west-to-east lines of communication (as opposed to the north-west and south-east line of the Peddars Way), and the construction of the necessary bridges, cuttings and embankments no doubt brought about further modifications to the road. It all gave added impetus to the movement away of people and goods, pushing the road even further into disuse and isolation. Thus in 1914 WG Clarke was able to comment that 'in places it (the road) is even now impassable to vehicular traffic owing to overhanging brambles, thickly-growing bracken, and treacherous rabbit-burrows.' In other words, by the latter part of the 19th century the Way had become a local backwater, its former importance being largely forgotten as it slipped gradually from memory into leafy obscurity.

There are fascinating 'snapshots' of the road between the years 1913 and 1944 to be seen in the marvellous pen and ink sketches of Frank Patterson, the cycling artist, many of whose illustrations formerly graced the pages of Cycling magazine. Some of his sketches suggest that during this period the road was still fairly well defined and in parts was being used by horses and presumably carriages, for a central groove cut in the grass by hooves is sometimes visible. One of his pictures is of the Way 'near Thompson,' possibly sketched in the 1920s when the area was still open heathland and there was not a conifer in sight. Another,

A view of the Way not far from Harpley as it strides on towards Holme and the coast. Farming interests dominate the landscape in this area

dated 1931, of a stretch between Roudham and Thompson, is captioned, 'A Norfolk road which is to be cleared, repaired and improved - alas!' This may have been the metalled road north of the Dog and Partridge at Wretham. Yet another glimpse of the Way is to be seen in BP's cycling notes published in the Eastern Evening News of October 23, 1946. He (or she) evidently pedalled off along the Way where it crosses the A11, and she (or he) found it all fairly easy going and easy to follow on the map. "There is some delightful scenery along here, particularly in the autumn, as it journeys on through Breckland, and I commend it to every cyclist who enjoys a run through secluded glades and over open stretches of country away from other traffic,' the article continued.

The writer warned against attempting the entire journey to the coast in a single day, adding that 'every mile discloses something, if not in scenery then in age-old history.' However, the track was inclined to the rough, and the best advice then, as now, was to take a puncture repair outfit. Interestingly, BP also particularly enjoyed 'picturesque spots like Thompson Water,' which suggests this stretch of the Way was not, at that stage, out of bounds to the public. But by this time another substantial landscape change was already taking place.

March of the forests

Death, deprivation and additional heavy demands on resources sapped the lifeblood of the nation during the second decade of the 20th century, and not even the landed gentry were immune. By the end of the First World War many large estates in England were in a parlous financial state, irrevocably damaged by social and political change and a lack of heirs, brought about by the chill winds of war. Low agricultural prices and low rents also drained their stamina, and those in areas of poor or indifferent soil, such as Breckland, were particularly badly affected. Many farms were left untenanted and land became derelict.

As early as 1916 the Government, and through them the Forestry Committee of the Ministry of Reconstruction, alarmed by the increasing demands of the war and worryingly depleted timber stocks, began to consider plans to develop and enlarge woodland resources, but it was not until 1922, four years after the conflict had ended, that the new Forestry Commission - attracted by low prices and an abundance of labour - made its first land purchases in Breckland.

This ultimately vast enterprise actually began with the acquisition of a small acreage near Swaffham. Then, with plenty of land still available, they turned their attention elsewhere, buying plots at Elveden on the Downham Hall estate, and at Lynford and Beechamwell, and so on. Indeed, so successful and expansive was the project that by 1939, a mere 18 years after they began, the Commission held 59,000 acres of Breckland. Of this, some three-quarters was owned freehold and the rest leased.

It would be foolish to suggest that the forestry enterprise did not have its critics - even throughout the 1960s and 1970s there were major grumbles about the onward and seemingly unending march of dark and dreary pines - but what cannot be denied, now that the outlines of the plantations have softened and the species are more varied, is that it has had a major impact upon the landscape of Breckland. It always has been a matter of balance. On one side the burgeoning plantations swallowed ancient heaths and mysterious dips and hollows by the lorry load, but as the trees grew and planting techniques and the selection of species became more enlightened, so the look of the Brecks changed.

Ironically, the activities of the area's great benefactors also sparked any number of disputes, often surrounding the Peddars Way and usually involving disagreements over obstructions, rights of way and legal status. In turn, regular references to the old road in the Eastern Daily Press invariably inspired fresh correspondence as to the road's origins, route and purpose. One letter some years ago, I recall, responded to a query over the Way's origins by suggesting the road was in fact little more than a badger run.

One of the most useful eruptions of wrath occurred in the 1930s when a fierce public debate was fuelled by the erection of a rash of gates which effectively blocked what had hitherto been thought of as long established public footpaths. At a meeting of the Rural District Council at Union House, Thetford, reported in the EDP on December 6, 1930, one indignant member proposed that at places where the Way crossed public roads noticeboards should be erected stating that the 'green road' was a public right of way. Referring to correspondence in the EDP, Mr P St JB Grigson said that at several places gates had been erected across the Way - one of the most interesting historical remains they had in Norfolk - along with 'Trespassers will be prosecuted' signs. The Way, he said, was a relic which should be kept for the people.

However, the clerk to the RDC revealed it was the council itself which had given the Forestry Commission permission to erect these gates on the understanding that they were not locked and that they would be removed within ten years. So after a long discussion the council finally decided to refer the entire matter of rights of way on the Peddars Way to the county council, and more specifically to the county surveyor. This was after they had turned down another member's presumably jocular suggestion that they should form a special sub-committee made up 'of the best walkers.'

So Thetford RDC quickly established that the culprits were indeed one of the area's newest employers, the Forestry Commission, and that it had been caused by their own lack of foresight in granting permission for the gates in the first place. No doubt they were also mindful of the Commission's substantial contribution to the local economy. Nevertheless, discontent hung in the air.

Fours years later, in February, 1934, the definitive report was finally made public, the daunting job of checking the entire route of the Way having been passed some time before to the highways (King's Lynn) committee of Norfolk County Council. It was given the task of deciding the legal status of the road by surveying the entire length of the old Roman road by dint of the careful examination of old documents and estate maps. This is what they did, and under the auspices of the clerk, HC Davies, it has to be said they did a remarkably thorough job. In effect their report,

published in the EDP in February, 1934, more or less confirmed and established the route we enjoy today.

The report commented: 'An axiom often quoted in connection with highway law is, Once a Highway always a Highway, and so far as roads of any kind have been used as public highways since English law and customs became crystallised in their present form, the axiom generally holds true, and for a very great number of years a highway could not be abolished as such except with certain legal formalities.' But the compilers also took the view that the axiom may have been abandoned centuries before, so that the final declarations as to status had to be the Inclosure Acts of the 18th and 19th centuries. It also concluded that the highways authority was not, in effect, responsible for repairs to the road.

The rest of the newspaper's report was a resume of the route and the related legal awards, all too numerous to mention here but which included:

Bridgham, 1806.

Roudham, 1773, leading 'across the Turnpike Road and Great Heath called Ridge Road or Pilgrim's Way.'

Hockham, 1798, south from Black Breck.

Tottington, 1774, Cherry Row Corner by Mad House.

Thompson, 1817, Cherry Row Corner by Mad House to the

Blackwater at Little Cressingham.

Little Cressingham, 1778, called Walsingham Way Road, south over the river at Hills Common and by the White House alehouse.

Ashill, 1786, called Walsingham Way.

Swaffham, 1869.

Sporle, 1806, referred to as Procession Lane.

Sedgeford, 1797, named Podder's Road (a possible mis-spelling).

Holme, 1827, Way north from county road in Holme 'not treated as repairable by the inhabitants.'

Towards the end of the much praised report some members appended the hope that it established beyond doubt that the public did have the right to walk the Peddars Way and that they should use it 'to prevent it being wholly absorbed into adjoining lands, as much of its length had been.' Another enthusiastic speaker said a copy of the report should be placed in the hands of every teacher.

But there were even noisier rumblings in the background. From the time of the First World War and even before, airmen and troops with their guns and machines had trained on the vast Breckland lands amid the shelter belts, so that

Right: A weather-beaten sign near Anmer Minque, on the way to Houghton

they were a not uncommon sight. Then in 1942, with the Second World War well under way, the War Department moved into the area with even greater force and authority, appropriating hundreds of acres to establish the Stanford Battle Area which, between Thompson and Watering Farm, came alongside and even across a particularly lovely stretch of the Roman road. With no through route available and the Second World War to worry about, the Way once again faded into the foliage.

History since 1950s

The concept of Long Distant Routes was created when a report by the Hobhouse Committee finally led to the 1949 National Parks and Access to the Countryside Act. By the early 1950s, however, society was largely obsessed with two other items aside from walking and the end of rationing. One was the car, the numbers of which exploded from about 1951 onwards - and which, incidentally, finally persuaded me to give up leisure cycling, because of traffic jams and the stink. The other, from 1953, was television. It was a phase everyone went through, and in consequence many out-door pursuits, including football and cricket, increasingly had to take something of a back seat. This left the Peddars Way and other many other paths to their own

thoughts and devices while they awaited the next fresh air fitness phase. So where the Way was actually useful to farmers and their vehicles, then grass and vegetation were kept in check. As for the lengths which were of little use and thus little used, they became the haunt of nettle and bramble, bird and rabbit, little creatures and overhanging branches.

But the legal status of the old road, or parts of it, remained a thorny problem for many years. For example, in 1951 East Harling magistrates dealt with a case involving two men brought before the court for poaching. A car had been searched by police on the Peddars Way at Bridgham, and two shotguns and three dead rabbits had been found. The defence solicitor argued that if the Way at Bridgham was not a highway then the police evidence was inadmissible. It was a matter the magistrates had to consider, and the chairman of the bench finally ruled thus: 'We believe, with our local knowledge, that there has been a highway there for many hundreds of years. It is unfortunate that it should have fallen into a track in certain places. In other places it is actually used as a highway, and we over-rule that objection.' According to the EDP of March 28, 1951, the men were duly found guilty and fined £2 for being found with the guns and rabbits and £2 each for pursuing conies

Marl pits litter the fields on both sides of the Way as the old road gets into its stride between Fring and Houghton. Picture by the Norfolk Museums and Archaeology Service

without a licence.

The first person I ever talked to who had actually walked the Norfolk length of the Way was Eric Fowler, the taciturn and wise feature and leader writer of the Eastern Daily Press who contributed the hugely popular Jonathan Mardle column every Wednesday morning. His walk was undertaken in 1959, some 14 years before my own interest was finally translated into physical effort, and in 1972 he recounted to me with considerable enthusiasm his tramp along the Way in the moonlight, taking his ease at nearby pubs, resting on a river bank listening to the water, and the grasping fronds of vegetation which regularly hampered his progress. Eric, who served abroad in the army during the Second World War, was also interested in the history of the road, lending his support to the ferry theory which was current at the time. But reading his articles again I am left with the impression that it was really the peace and solitude he sought and remembered, not the conspiratorial whisperings of the ancients.

Anyway, carrying a rucksack full of spare clothes and clad in an 'ordinary pair of thick shoes,' it took him six days to walk the 50 miles or so from Ixworth to Holme. During that hot August week along the road in 1959 he found that parts of the Way had been ploughed over while other sections were still traceable 'as a flinty lane running between hedgerows of oak, ash, hazel, thorn and crab apple; a green way, raised above the neighbouring fields, and much encroached upon by brambles.' In places it was 36ft wide, at others 45ft wide. Most nights he left the track to find a lodging for the night, except one night when 'in defiance of the War Office I slept out under a clump of hawthorns alongside the Way where it passes through the Stanford training area.' He made himself a couch of bracken and slept soundly, being woken by the crump and rattle of a mock battle somewhere in the training area and by the sound of every cock pheasant in the neighbourhood. 'It was very beautiful at sunset,' he wrote, 'when an owl drifted in his ghostly fashion out of the woods and across the darkening sky ... The sunrise was beautiful, too, with the rays from the eastward glancing through the trees, dew on the bracken, and hares racing across the fields.'

Eric recorded that he made no new historical discoveries, but he delighted 'over the itch to explore' and remembered with gratitude the cottager who offered him two glasses of deliciously cold well-water and then let him clamber over her back garden fence into Barningham Park, where he found a grassy mound, 45 ft across and shaded by splendid oaks, running straight across the park. It was his first glimpse of the old road proper.

Trouble visited the Way again in the 1960s when farming was in another of its expansionist moods. In 1967 some hedgerows were slashed, burned and levelled near Great Massingham and Harpley Common, and in 1969 more thorn and crab apple hedges were torn out so that fields could be ploughed right to the very edge. This time there were protests in the local Press, and even the noted naturalist, EA (Ted) Ellis, was moved to enter the fray. He was livid. So was Norfolk County Council, which later re-marked the verges with concrete posts. But the hedgerows, alas, were gone.

It is worth remembering that for 30 years after the Second World War the contemplation of a walk along the Peddars Way was as far as most people got, for at the Breckland end of the route there was another formidable obstacle in addition to the general obscurity of the road. The presence and regular activities of the military meant that until well into the 1970s there was a barrier and sentry box, and occasionally a sentry, across the Way at Stowbedon Plantation just south of Thompson Water. And near Sparrow Hill, the Battle Area spilled across and on both sides of the Roman road, as it still does today.

Entreaties to the Army to have the barriers lifted and the Way completely re-opened to the public were rejected on a number of occasions, usually on the grounds that, first, military exercises were held regularly over the land hereabouts, and second, that the landscape was littered with unexploded shells and other dangerous bits of ordnance. The first excuse was certainly true, for it was not uncommon during this period, and indeed for some time afterwards, for walkers to be confronted by or even delayed by troops in full battle dress, or even by armoured vehicles. Not until nearer the middle of the decade did public opinion finally force a change; but eventually the barrier was dismantled by the Ministry of Defence and the sentries, after a time, disappeared. For some time afterwards, however, troops would still pop out of the undergrowth near the track, menacing and sometimes even lost. You would see riflemen lurking behind the trees or find piles of spent shells beside the track. But you are much less likely to see anything save helicopters now.

Nevertheless, until 1975 it was necessary for walkers heading north along the Way to divert away from the Peddars Way, turning instead past cottages and Watering Farm - where I once also enjoyed some deliciously cold water straight from a well - and completing a complicated, unofficial and somewhat lengthy detour which often incorporated the disused Stow Bedon railway track beside Thompson Common and then back through Thompson village.

This was the backdrop against which I made my first tentative forays along the Peddars Way, undertaken in the early 1970s in the manner of expeditions of discovery and as week-long exercises. It was a fascinating but not particularly easy undertaking. There was no definable or official route. There were precious few signposts and no guidebooks and therefore no suitable maps drawn specifically for walkers. We invented our own routes, even though we did not always know where private land ended and public areas began. Nor were there any official camp sites or bed and breakfast establishments, but instead, a lot of skulking over corners of private land and illicit overnight tenting hidden among Forestry Commission trees, on the edge of the Battle Area, or behind farm hedges. In those days it was the only option.

Nor were some of the pubs particularly welcoming to walkers, who they saw as muddy itinerants of doubtful origin and a very real threat to the much more lucrative sports car trade. In one or two places the discrimination lingered a long time. One well-known pub in North West Norfolk, now a regular stopping place for yompers, back in the 1970s insisted that walkers jettisoned their boots at the front door - it still abhors mud, and has a notice to say so - and then use a side bar separate from the well-dressed jet-setters and society sailors sipping their Pimms in the lounge.

Remember, too, there were no catwalks over the boggy bits or even footbridges over the rivers. Slopping through the mud and wading the muddy-bottomed and thigh-deep Little Ouse and Thet rivers became the order of the day. Nor was the route always in good condition. More often than not we saw no other walkers, aside from occasional short stretches where people exercised their dogs, and in some places the vegetation, unhindered by passing farm vehicles, grew apace. One section not far from Anmer was invariably blocked by nettles and brambles and was a real battle to get through.

Nevertheless, I was fascinated by it all. But again, there appeared to be no general history of the Peddars Way on Norwich library shelves to tell me more about it, and no real attempt that I could find to explain who had built the road, and more intriguingly, when and why. I wanted to know more, and began with a well-thumbed copy of Rainbird Clarke's East Anglia, written in 1960, which actually contained nothing specific about the road at all and which in some respects, I came to realise, was out-of-date even then. So I began my own notes and kept my own files, jotting down every reference I came across.

One factor which did help the gradual re-emergence of the Way from relative obscurity was a change of heart by the Forestry Commission. Instead of exhibiting 'No Admittance' notices in profusion and maintaining a public face of fierce determination to hold back the tides of those wanting to enter and enjoy the forests, the signs slowly began to change to those of 'Circular Walk' and 'Picnic Area.' Hostility against the public began to evaporate and leisure parks and walks evolved and proliferated to the extent that for the last 25 years, and perhaps for longer, the forests of the Brecks, including the southern end of Norfolk's Peddars Way, have been a major leisure attraction and an invaluable green lung. In 1990 the entire Thetford Forest was designated a Forest Park. Set against the earlier loss of so many acres of ancient heathland, the plantations have made their own individualistic contribution to the area and made useful and beautiful many acres of otherwise sandy, flinty and difficult farm land.

In 1982 there were more arguments over the status of the road when car rally organisers announced they were planning to use part of the track near Fring, a prospect which sparked another spirited debate and which acted as a reminder that parts of the Way were still classified as highway and thus could be used by motor vehicles. It also underlined the thought that the old Roman road had remained for many decades largely isolated from modern transport corridors, the grinding uphill stretch from Castle Acre to Shepherd's Bush being one obvious exception.

Of course, there were still more arguments to come, because the thoughts of leisure planners and enthusiasts were also beginning to turn towards the possible creation of a long distance walking route across Norfolk. But before I tell you about that, and thus leave the actual history of the old road forever, a few more places of interest and importance, which can be seen and enjoyed along the Way, need to be mentioned.

Other features along the Way

Across the rivers and into the trees

Crossing streams and rivers safely and relatively easily must have been an early preoccupation, and one can imagine that the discovery of a shallow crossing place was a prized piece of information. With uninhibited rivers rising and falling and moving back and forth across their floodplains, unbanked and unchecked, there may have been more shallow places than are apparent today. Thus those used on a regular basis would soon become well-known and quickly develop into a local focus for tracks and perhaps settlement. But for the Romans, fords must have presented a different set of problems. Whereas wandering tracks might quite easily twist and turn to reach the best crossings, placing engineered roads on a precise course for the best fords without the routes losing an immediate sense of direction, must have been a difficult art.

Even so, and despite the fact that the Peddars Way crossed innumerable waterways (the Little Ouse, Thet, Watton Brook, East Wretham, and the Wissey, Nar and Heacham rivers, for example) there is no evidence to suggest that the surveyors who laid it out had to resort to the building of bridges on a regular basis. Far from it. The only slight evidence - a possible suggestion of timber baulks - of a bridge on the Way is over the Watton Brook at Saham Toney, near Woodcock Hall. Claims are often made for various constructions across the Thet at Thorpe Farm near Brettenham, but no conclusive evidence has been found. However, it may be significant that both sites - Saham Toney/Threxton, and Brettenham (which some experts suggest back-translates to the name Bretta, or even 'the

Right: Carved bench end of a pedlar in Swaffham church

Briton') - were the localities of substantial and presumably important Romano-British or Iron Age settlements about which, at the time of writing, agonisingly little is known but which, one suspects, were widely influencial and probably played a significant role in this particular tale.

I have no idea how the Romans crossed the Heacham river at Fring, the Nar, or even the Wissey, unless they simply rode or waded across, but these, and the crossing places at Knettishall (Blackwater ford, which marks the boundary between Suffolk and Norfolk) and Brettenham (Droveway ford) have been in existence a very long time. The 'hardening' of these latter two fords by the judicious placing of large stones has been proposed in the past, and indeed it would seem to have been a quite logical thing to do were it not for the fact that, in most places in Norfolk, suitable stone is in very limited supply.

A slight mis-alignment of the Way on both sides of the rivers at Blackwater and Droveway fords hint that the Romans might have made use of a sort of Z-bend to increase the dispersement of traffic crossing what must

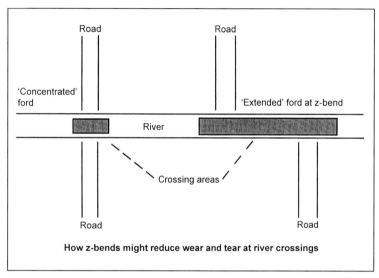

How z-bends might reduce wear and tear at river crossings

have been wet and muddy environments. If this was the case it seems most likely to have occurred at Brettenham, though once again, the proximity of a substantial settlement on the banks of the river may have necessitated what seems to have been minor adjustments to the road.

Droveway and Blackwater fords both appear on the maps

of Faden (1797) and Bryant (1826), although they are not named on Bryant and are drawn to look somewhat less important. Faden, in marking additional converging tracks in the neighbourhood, particularly near Blackwater ford, clearly implies they still had some useful status towards the end of the 18th century. In the 1970s, when I waded both rivers in the proximity of the two fords, my bare feet detected no stones, but I did sink up to my knees in soft, black mud which took a long time to disperse in the slow moving waters. It occurred to be then that perhaps this might have been one of the origins of the oft-recurring river and stream name, Black Water.

Knettishall Heath country park (Suffolk)
Over 370 acres of Breck heath, river access, mixed woodland plantations, picnic areas and grassland. It is a start/finish point for the Peddars Way and the Angles Way walks, while the Icknield Way route joins (or leaves) the network here, too.

Brettenham Heath nature reserve (English Nature)
One of the largest blocks of heathland left in Breckland. There are areas of heath and grass, in some places replaced by bracken and invaded by birch and hawthorn scrub. And lots of rabbits. Because of the reserve's importance and fragility, access is restricted. And while we are in the area, Thetford Forest Park now embraces about 50,000 acres of pine forest and heathland and broadleaf areas.

Harling Drove (or Great Fen Road)
The route, which crosses the Peddars Way immediately north of the railway level crossing close to the A11, seems to have begun at Blackdike, not far from Hockwold, and may once have led to the sea. Inland, it suggests a continuation towards East Harling. The road's origins are doubtful and it is possible the route is not Iron Age or even Roman, but medieval, in which case it may have tracked marginally south to avoid the Larling 'swamps,' to re-connect with the Roman road near Harling and other medieval routes to Norwich. There is much uncertainty, though it seems it was once used by geese and turkey drovers.

Grimes Graves
The region's first large-scale industrial site. The indentations are Neolithic flint mines which were re-examined in the 1870s when over 300 pits and shafts were discovered. The Icknield Way may have been used to aid distribution of these high grade tools.

East Wretham heath (Norfolk Wildlife Trust)
About 360 acres of grassland, heath and woodland. There are pine plantations and meres. A lovely spot.

Around the bend
Viewed from the ground rather than on a map, the Way is not straight but made up of straight sections. What is remarkable is the general accuracy of the surveyors' sightings in plotting a track for the road from Suffolk, across Norfolk, and to the very place on the coast where, plainly, they wanted to be. Again, on the ground, the Way does make a number of minor directional adjustments, though these may have been because of local considerations such as wet, insecure ground or other physical barriers. But it appears to make only one actual navigational shift, at Galley Hill, between East Wretham and Merton which, significantly perhaps, is on marginally higher ground than the surrounding landscape and so may have been used as a sighting point. We must guard against too much excitement, however. Neither Faden nor Bryant make much of the bend and indeed portray it as little more than a subtle curve. What is equally plain is that there have been substantial changes to the roads and tracks in this area over the years, presumably because of forestry, the military

and agriculture. Thus the presently perceived line of the Peddars Way may be a greatly amended version of the original.

Water, everywhere
Thompson Water, despite its delightful reed-fringed, rustic appearance, is a comparatively modern addition to the local environment. The tributary of the Wissey which crosses the Way here was once an important ford and watering place for travellers and stock, and there was a sheepwash in the vicinity. Much of the land hereabouts was enclosed in about 1817, and in 1845 the tributary was blocked and allowed to flood, creating the lake. There is a story that the 'tumuli' east of the Way near Thompson Water is little more than a spoil heap from the lake diggings.

Thompson common and carr (Norfolk Wildlife Trust)
Over 300 acres, embracing a huge diversity of flowering plants. A mosaic of grasses, pingos (shallow pools formed at the end of the last Ice Age), scrub and woodland. Another delightful place.

Headless travellers
In his 1925 book In Breckland Wilds, the writer WG Clarke

recounted a number of ghost stories, including one closely allied to the Peddars Way. A spectre, he said, was recorded as having haunted the road between Threxton and Saham Toney, otherwise Dark Lane close to Woodcock Hall. "It consists," he wrote, "of a carriage noiselessly drawn by four headless horses, with several headless persons seated on the box. . . . Those that have seen it have recognised in these headless beings the forms of certain of their deceased friends." Strangely, when Robin Brown wrote about the story in the parish magazine The Saham Saga a few years ago, a gentleman from Watton telephoned to say that 70 years before, as a young boy standing by the bridge near Threxton church, he actually saw the apparition.

Barrows, little and large
The Little Cressingham group, to the west of the Peddars Way, consists of six known barrows and one ring ditch. When excavators got stuck into one of them in 1849 they uncovered a male skeleton, the skull apparently displaying 'a large development of the animal passion.' Whatever that is. Grave goods recovered included a bronze dagger and knife, a gold breast plate, three gold boxes, fragments of a gold mount and an amber necklace, all of a type classified as Wessex Culture. Another site was examined in 1977,

when it was found that although no actual barrow survived it had once been surrounded by two ditches. One of the sites was known as Bell Hill, as local tradition asserted that parish church bells were buried there.

A further seven barrows visible from the Peddars Way are at Harpley Common and Anmer Minque. They may form the southern end of a group possibly numbering as many as fourteen which stand on the chalk ridge separating the headwaters of the Wensum and Babingley rivers. Three of the Harpley barrows were dug in 1843, revealing layers of bone and charcoal - possibly representing secondary insertions - while another was excavated in 1973. Dispersed cremated bone and sherds were found. Charcoal from beneath the mound gave a date of about 1770BC.

Medieval wonders
St Mary's church at Houghton-on-the-Hill, not far from North Pickenham, used to be a tree shielded ivy-clad ruin of a building shunned by almost everyone but near-do-wells. Then in 1992 a remarkable restoration programme was begun. The site was cleared and the building restored, and it was then that a series of extraordinary 10th or 11th century wall paintings were discovered. The pictures, depicting Heaven and the Resurrection, together with a

huge representation of the Trinity on the east wall, are now believed to be the earliest examples of their kind in Europe. Other churches in the area may well have boasted similar adornments, but St Mary's seems to represent a sole survivor. Excavation on the lonely hilltop also pinpointed a possible 7th century burial ground and two skeletons thought to have been buried when an earlier, presumably timber, Saxon structure stood on the spot. One wonders what effect the paintings would have have on pilgrims passing back and forth on their way to and from Walsingham.

Fact and fiction
A well-known folk tale associated with Swaffham, which is but a brisk walk from the Way. Indeed, Swaffham church has some wonderful bench-end carvings, some of which represent a pedlar. The story tells of a pedlar who dreamed that if he travelled to London he would be told where he might find his fortune. To cut a long story short, he did and he was. All of which seems a marvellous cover story for someone suddenly coming into possession of a great deal of additional finance and in desperate need of an

Right: Looking south, as the Way approaches Fring crossroads. Note the width

explanation. However, subsequent research has shown there was a certain John Chapman (chapman is an old name meaning pedlar, or barter-man) who paid for the erection of Swaffham's north aisle following a masonry collapse in 1454. Whether or not there was such a man who went to London, and whether or not he did make use of the Way for at least part of his journey, remains firmly within in the realm of speculation. Nevertheless, a simularity in name, allied to Swaffham's proximity to the Way, means that the road and the legend are often mentioned in more or less the same breath. (See also: Evolution and change)

The Way obscured
The actual line of the Way on the surface of the landscape immediately south of Castle Acre is obscure - though cropmarks have been recorded - and disappeared generations ago. But the Nar crossing place, from an early military point of view, ought to have been a strategically important location, the more so because the Nar may also have been navigable from the sea. Surprisingly little Roman material has emerged from this small hilltop town, one of the most attractive and tourist-visited in Norfolk. It is at least possible the Way and its original line within the settlement was obliterated or modified during the construction of de

Warenne's castle and bailey and the laying out of the street pattern. The subsequent construction of a Cluniac priory would have ensured even more traffic along the Way.

Marling mania
North of Castle Acre, as the Way approaches some of its longest and loneliest stretches, the walker will begin to notice scatters of pits which pockmark the fields on either side. They can be mistaken for ponds or even, if they are disguised by clumps of trees, as barrows; but in reality, most of them are the remnants of marl pits. North of Breckland the landscape changes to a vista of dry, rolling uplands, known as the Good Sands, for it was discovered that by judicious digging to the clayey calcerous subsoil below, and by spreading this substance across the fields, some of the acidity was neutralised and the soil structure was improved. There are said to be references to marling in Breckland and around Holkham in the 14th century, and it was adopted on a large scale in the 18th and 19th centuries, particularly within the catchment areas of the Raynham, Holkham and Houghton estates. Without doubt it was a labour intensive and filthy job, carried out in the winter when there was a shortage of other work and the fields were empty of crops. In wet weather it must have been

particularly difficult for the men, horses and carts. The technique became less common after about 1850 as labour costs increased and coal became cheaper, and when lime was used for much the same purpose.

Magazine Cottage
The Peddars Way runs directly beside the somewhat unusual Magazine Cottage at Sedgeford, which was originally built as a powder store and armoury about 1640.

A ritual landscape? (part two)
As mentioned earlier, it may be a misnomer to describe West and North West Norfolk in the Bronze and Iron Ages as a ritual landscape, inasmuch that today's Norfolk landscape cannot really be described as 'ritual' either, despite the fact that it is stippled with the outlines of hundreds of parish churches. Yet there are enough significant reasons to at least allude to the use of such a label. For example, during the Bronze Age the so-called Seahenge timbers, latterly and controversially salvaged from their site on the present beach at Holme, may well have been only one such structure in a landscape which in those days evidently extended seaward for a considerable distance. During the Iron Age, too, there was also established the extraordinary deposition site at Ken Hill, Snettisham, which has produced dozens of torcs from dozens of pits and which clearly had influence over a very wide area. And in the south, just outside Thetford and right on the line of the Icknield Way, was the extraordinary Fison Way/Gallows Hill site, excavated by the late Tony Gregory. This timber construction of puzzling intricacy and immense scale, which was destroyed or perhaps removed in the aftermath of the Boudican uprising, seems to have been of significance to the local Iceni. But there were other, smaller places, too.

At Ashill, about three miles from the Peddars Way, a 12-acre ditch and bank site constructed in the Claudio-Neronian period (circa AD 47 to AD 61) and occupied until at least the late second century, was examined in the 1870s and again in 1961. In an area once known as Robin Hood's Garden, the site actually came to light in 1874 during the construction of the Watton and Swaffham railway line. In the 1970s, after re-examining evidence from the digs, Tony Gregory suggested the bank and ditch arrangement might represent a native defensive structure thrown up during the revolt, or perhaps an internal security measure built during the client-kingship of Prasutagus (circa AD 47-60). However, the discovery of three wells, or shafts, one almost 40 feet deep and timbered all the way down, and carefully and deliberately filled with eleven individual deposits of pottery vessels embedded in organic material, suggested it was more likely the enclosure was constructed specifically for ritual purposes. Much of the site evidently survived the destructive aftermath of the Boudican revolt, and buildings were added at some point. It was then absorbed into agricultural activities, and what remained of the rampart was levelled in the third or fourth century.

In 1990 a partially dispersed hoard of 153 silver Iceni coins was found at Fring beside the Peddars Way not far from the known site of a probable Roman villa - a short distance to the east of the Way - and a ditched enclosure beside the Way, to the west. A tesselated floor at the Romano-British villa site had been recorded 200 years earlier, while aerial photographs showed the ditched enclosure had at least three divided areas and traces of structures. The coins had been placed in a pot sealed by a piece of cloth perhaps tied over the mouth, and studies suggested the hoard had been buried at around the time of the Boudican revolt. Fring parish is next door to Snettisham parish - with its possible metal-working site and deposited torcs - and the entire area seems to have exuded wealth during the Iron Age. It is at least possible that a trade-orientated settlement may have existed near to the Way in this part of Norfolk prior to the revolt, the hoard reflecting local wealth and social influence. A alternative interpretation is that the large numbers of metal artefacts in the area might instead represent votive deposits. While this is thought unlikely in the case of the Fring hoard, it is certainly very possible throughout the rest of the area.

Space-age Sedgeford

Walkers on the Peddars Way heading north all know the place where the Way crosses the Heacham river and the narrow lane into Sedgeford, at Fring Cross, because it is at this point they have to decide whether to continue the journey to the coast or detour into the village for a stop at the pub. An intensive long-term study of the historic and prehistoric development of the parish began in 1995, with the expectation it might last 20 years. Most of the work is concentrated in three areas in and around the village, and studies so far have been assisted by the American National Space Agency and some high-tec geophysics. The Sedgeford Historical & Archaeological Research Project (SHARP for short) is important not only in a local context but it is also a test-bed for new and emerging research techniques. Experts also hope to answer the questions:

One of the most dramatic views of the Way as it reaches Fring Cross, in the valley, and then curves over the hill towards the clump of trees at the top, its progress marked by the line of hedge

when did English people begin living in villages, and was it a free choice to abandon earlier 'dispersed' settlements.

Ringstead Downs (Norfolk Wildlife Trust)

Just to the west of the Way as it prepares to enter Ringstead is an area known as Ringstead Downs, close by Hunstanton Park, which at first glance looks as though it might be a series of manmade ramparts. The feature sits right on the edge of what is known as the limit of Devensian drift (geologically speaking, Hunstanton Till) which was left behind by the last glaciation. The Ringstead Downs valley cuts into the chalk to a depth of 10 to 13 metres below the plateau surface, and once formed part of a lake which extended east of the village. The lake filled until it overflowed, the water bursting through the chalk, spilling southwest and carving the steep-sided valley in the process. It is now a rare example of Norfolk chalk grassland.

Ringstead root and branch

The actual shape and line of the Way as it approaches the sea near Holme has never been satisfactorily determined, because so much of the seaward landscape has been lost and because possible variations have not been conclusively

Right: Fring Cross and the crossing of the Heacham river

mapped. It is assumed that side roads connected the Way with the Icknield Way and the line of Roman period country houses, and possibly with Brancaster, and it is often held that a further branch road curved westward from the Way at Ringstead roughly in the direction of Old Hunstanton. Also in the vicinity is Green Bank, a track thought to be very old and possibly dating from the Iron Age; while three quite different roads seem to lead into Holme. The centre road, signposted Peddars Way, carries today's traffic. This is wrong, as all the evidence suggests the actual original line of the Way is that slightly to the west which, appropriately enough, is actually incorporated in Norfolk's National Trail. This line, if continued, also leads straight to the beach. A possible third connection is a (presently fragmented) line of tracks running roughly north from Bluestone Farm which actually cross over Green Bank.

Holme Dunes/Bird Observatory (Norfolk Wildlife Trust, Norfolk Ornithologists' Association)
Two major reserves. There is a boardwalk through the dunes and lots of plants to see. The observatory boasts over 320 species of birds recorded since 1962, and over 50 species of flora.

A new National Trail

A long distance walking route across Norfolk was first suggested by Norfolk County Council as long ago as 1969, twenty years after the 1949 National Parks and Access to the Countryside Act, but a major problem soon emerged. One of many subsequent problems, it has to be said. Then, however, Norfolk's length of the Peddars Way, about 45 miles, was quite simply too short for inclusion in the Countryside Commission's long distance trail category. The solution, Norfolk realised, was to join it to another newly devised path, which duly became known as the Coast Path and which ran from Hunstanton to Cromer. The pair pushed the mileage total to about 93 miles. And so after a great deal of discussion and consultation - and a not inconsiderable amount of opposition, some of it surprisingly ferocious - the county finally agreed, in 1974, to actively promote the idea.

Consultations between the Countryside Commission (now the Countryside Agency), the county council and various other bodies finally took place, and tacit agreement was ultimately given to the development of this or a similar route. To this end a feasibility study was finally undertaken between 1978 and 1980 for the Commission and other interested parties by JF (Willie) Wilson, a field officer

employed for the purpose by Norfolk County Council.
Over the next few months Willie did all the necessary leg-
work, massaged bruised egos, wrote pleading letters, made
friendly phone calls, pacified antagonistic farmers and
bristling landowners - who seemed to anticipate avalanches
of drunken litter louts rampaging through pheasant breed-
ing areas, frightening the horses and leaving paddock gates
open - attended countless meetings, and soothed the brows
of concerned parish councils.

When his consultation paper was published in January,
1980, the difficulties he had faced immediately became
clear. For example, he and his fellow planners had been
forced to deal with two county councils, four district
councils, six parish meetings, 51 parish councils and 16
other bodies and Government departments. In addition, 20
of the 37 landowners involved had lodged objections to the
plan, or elements of it. They all had to be allowed their say.
For the record, and at 1979 prices, capital outlay for the
establishment of the route was estimated at £61,000, with
an annual outlay of £2400.

Finally, in August, 1981, the entire scheme was submitted
for approval to the Secretary of State for the Environment,
and three months later a Peddars Way Association was
launched at an inaugural meeting at Swaffham attended by
more than 100 people. This was a voluntary organisation -
run enthusiastically by George and Jeanne le Surf, two
untiring, lifelong footpaths supporters - formed specifically
to promote and oversee the development of the route and to
produce an accommodation guide, tasks it successfully
completed for a number of years until, its initial targets
achieved, it was wound up in March, 1996. Some of its
duties were then taken on by the Ramblers' Association.

In October, 1982, the Secretary of State signalled his
approval of plans for the new route, and detailed planning
began in earnest, though sadly without Willie Wilson, who
died suddenly. In December, 1983, Willie's Clump, a small
group of native trees planted beside the Peddars Way near
Thompson Water, was dedicated to the memory of JF
Wilson.

There was more hectic activity in 1985 when the first
official guidebook, backed by the Countryside Commission
and Her Majesty's Stationary Office, was researched and
written by myself and put together by the Central Office of
Information. It was finally published in 1986, since when it
has been revised and reprinted several times.

In the end the period of time between approval of the final
report and the actual official opening was reassuringly
short. Some trails were not so fortunate. The North Corn-

wall Coast Path took 21 years from approval to opening, and the Pembrokeshire Coast Path 17 years. Better comparisons, perhaps, are the Ridgeway (one year) and the Pennine Way (14 years). The Peddars Way and Norfolk Coast Path was approved in October, 1982, and launched in July, 1986, a few months under four years. In the circumstances it was very quick indeed. Not much more than a decade had passed since the first serious move to establish a path had been made.

The Peddars Way and Norfolk Coast Path was finally declared open by the Prince of Wales one bright, blustery day in a ceremony witnessed by several hundred enthusiasts gathered amid the dunes on Holme beach. Afterwards many of us walked, together with the Prince, along the beach to Old Hunstanton. Among the well-known faces also present that day were Lord Melchett of Courtyard Farm, Ringstead, a great supporter of the trail idea, and comedian and writer Mike Harding, then representing the Ramblers' Association.

Today, this well loved and now throughly established National Trail - the label having been changed from Long Distance Route in 1989 - also incorporates bridle path sections while the walkers' trail is connected (at Knettishall) to the Ridgeway trail by the Icknield Way.

Also, by using the framework of the Peddars Way and the Norfolk Coast Path, walkers can complete a 230-mile circle of the county by incorporating the Weavers Way (Cromer to Yarmouth) and Angles Way (Yarmouth to Knettishall) paths.

The Way today

The combined length of the Peddars Way and Norfolk Coast Path National Trail route is about 93 miles, which makes it longer than the Wolds Way (83 miles) or the Ridgeway (86 miles), but generally at the shorter end of the pantheon of Countryside Agency approved paths in England and Wales. The Norfolk length of the Roman road itself is about 45 miles, but calculating footpath mileages is never a precise art because of differences between historical and modern lines, and more particularly, trail detours. So it is probably best to be somewhat hazy on the subject. There is also the question of kilometres, but as I have never walked one I am not the best person to ask.

At this point it is necessary to remind the reader that the old road is not confined entirely within the boundaries of Norfolk, but that it extends at least another four miles into Suffolk, to Stanton Chare, where it once joined another Roman road which seems to have headed roughly southwest through Stanton and Ixworth and north-east through East Harling and on, perhaps, to Crownthorpe (near Wymondham). Truth to tell there is little to be seen of the Way between Knettishall Heath and Stanton Chare other than a possible section appropriated by the Icknield Way trail (sections of an agger can still be seen in the undergrowth) and traces, so I am told, at Coney Weston and Barningham Park. On the whole, though, its progress in Suffolk is somewhat indistinct.

The best place to begin to experience the Peddars Way today is at Knettishall Heath, for there it still is, that gentle rise in the ground among the belt of trees to the west of and just behind the rails of the little car park at the Rushford end of the heath. The great military road has withered into a slight and almost indistinct hump in the grass, sometimes camouflaged by a carpet of leaves. As for the Peddars Way section of the national trail, it offers only a brief backward glance at Suffolk before evolving into a grassy path through a tunnel of green which immediately plunges into woodland. After some 800 yards it meanders over a narrow wooden footbridge across the river Little Ouse and into Norfolk.

This is Blackwater Ford, the former meeting place of several old paths, where thirty years ago, before the bridge was built and the route was designated, my companions and I waded across with our boots tied around our necks, rucksacks held high, and our legs wallowing thigh-high in sucking black mud. Eventually we all got across, our struggles leaving a long, weaving black stain of churned mud in the water. In the days when fords were used on a daily basis, and with people and animals constantly crossing, floating clouds of disturbed water must have been fairly commonplace and more noticeable in some places than others.

Beyond the bridge the Way passes, to the east, a recently excavated lake and then skirts the edges of a shelter-belt. There are lines of beech and spindle trees, and at particular times of the year the branches are sometimes festooned with drapes of cobwebs and millions of caterpillars. It can be an extraordinary and unexpected sight. The remnants of two or three parish boundary markers should also be hereabouts, too, but I could not find them there last time I was there. Either they are lost or they were covered by vegetation. Otherwise, this is a typical Breckland vista of shelter-belts, plantations, and sandy, flinty fields.

Once over the A1066 Thetford-Diss road the route enters Triangle Covert, formed by the junction of two roads, to the west, and the line of a disused connecting road. This

A faint light coloured line towards the top of the field horizon marks the route of the Peddars Way on one of its 'missing' sections, at Ringstead. The picture was taken, after a heavy downpour, in October as the field was being ploughed

apparently redundant piece of highway was some years ago used as temporary gravel store, presumably by the highway authorities, but all this has now been cleared away. It has also created an interesting phenomenon in that the surface of the disused stretch of road has almost disappeared. As you walk the narrow line where others have walked before you there are, admittedly, occasional glimpses of crumbling asphalt. But in truth a thick mossy, weedy carpet has encroached to such an extent it would be quite easy never to know there was ever a road here at all and that much of the hard surface actually survives, albeit under the green-ery. It demonstrates how quickly nature reclaims its own. The route goes over the Thetford-East Harling road and leads on into woodland vistas of mixed conifer and beech, the old Roman line now becoming the western boundary of the Thorpe Woodlands camping and caravan site, otherwise known as Thorpe Farm. Once again the agger reappears, this time on left where it is a gentle, grassy rise crowned by bushes and trees. Further along the track, as it moves ever closer to the river Thet, the walkers' route traverses the old river floodplain - now a dense tangle of boggy habitats - on a boardwalk which has been laid a few yards east of the agger. The boardwalk takes you safely over the mud and on towards the river bank. The old agger, now camouflaged by a jungle of wayward vegetation, appears to peter out close to the present river bank, and yet the road it still gives every impression of having been raised up, suggesting that the Romans, too, liked to keep their feet relatively dry.

At the river the path turns right along the bank and then left over another footbridge. The Thet is reed-fringed and narrow and often, especially after heavy rain, it has the consistency of brown soup, whereas 30 years ago it was so clear it was possible to watch fish feeding on the bottom among gently swaying fronds. Then it was beautiful, mirror-like and sunlit. But the area still has great appeal, and it is still historically productive, sites of Iron Age, Romano-British and medieval settlements littering the leafy vicinity. You can see the agger again on the edge of Broom Covert on the far side of the Bridgham road. In Broom Covert and along the shelter-belts the raised line of the old road has been cut in one or two places by farm machinery to effect new field exits and entrances, but eventually it runs beside Brettenham Heath National Nature Reserve, one of the largest areas of surviving Breckland heath (apart from areas still within the Battle Area) in Norfolk. Here, from behind the fence - entry into the reserve is restricted - you can see squillions of rabbits, scattered clumps of hawthorn, bracken and birch. A landscape something like this might have been slightly familiar to the Iceni.

Once over and away from the mad roar of the A11 the walker crosses the Thetford-Norwich railway line either by a level crossing or by a low, dank underpass. Almost immediately the Harling Drove Road sweeps in from the west, going who knows where on its unknown way. The by Roudham Heath and a gas repeater station, and on through another leafy corridor over the Illington road into Wretham, or Stonebridge as it is sometimes called, depending on which side of the road you are standing. Here the original line of the Way was obliterated many years ago by railway construction and the building of embankments and a railway bridge - now a ruin - and any number of realignments to the main road as it crosses a stream.

By the Dog & Partridge pub, beloved by generations of squaddies from the nearby Battle Area barracks, and about a mile along a hard surface military road to Galley Hill, the metalled route veers away and disappears into the army area while the Way continues as a rough track. It was at Galley Hill that Roman surveyors seem to have made a course adjustment to the north-west, establishing a fresh line which continues more or less unchanged all the way to the coast, still some 35 miles away.

The track from Galley Hill, which is plainly substantially modified and has clearly been repaired at various times by lorryloads of shingle and stone, often runs the gauntlet of the army battle area to the left and open farm land to the right. Ironically, behind the MoD fences a marvellous, beautiful wilderness survives. Helicopters chop-chop overhead and occasional live rounds crump and thump in the backround. But for all this, it is a delightful stretch. In summer, butterflies smother the sunlit verges of the old road and the area is dominated by tall trees, distant heaths and plantations, and parched, sandy fields. Even the reed-fringed Thompson Water is an oasis of calm. Conceived and dug in Victorian times, when a tributary of the river Wissey was stopped up, the lake is now a favourite haunt of duck and fishermen. Resting walkers can also be found hereabouts on hot days, too, while nearby is Willie Wilson's memorial plantation, affectionally known as Willie's Clump. This area, one might seriously suggest, is the heart of present-day Breckland. Incidentally, Faden's map marks the feeder stream which crosses the Way to enter the present Thompson Water as a ford, and it also marks a nearby site as Tottington Water.

Once by Madhouse Plantation, across the old Thompson to Tottington road and by Shakers Furze, the shadowy shape of a low agger is visible a few yards to the east. Over

Sparrow Hill, however, a zig-zag of estate paths lead you on through Merton Park, enabling the walker to emerge on Watton-Bodney road. Hereabouts is a missing stretch of the Peddars Way, long lost by all accounts, which seems to have once crossed the fields towards Woodcock Hall and then progressed over the stream and through the former Iron Age and Romano-British settlements. Alas, the walker has to divert into Little Cressingham and by Houghton Farm, and the old line of the Way does not really become visible again until Procession Lane, north of North Pickenham. This is a delightful, almost secretive stretch of grassy path, sometimes muddy, the gateway to which used to be a bridge carrying the old railway line.

It occurs to me when I walk here that, first, there was a Roman road; then there was a railway embankment and a large brick bridge; then the railway closed down, forcing the bridge and the embankment into redundancy and the bridge into ruin; then the bridge remnants and the railway embankment were systematically dismantled; and now the old Roman road has become the pre-eminent line of communication once again. Procession Lane in summer can be very beautiful, grassy and hedged, a sunken corridor occasionally criss-crossed by paths once walked by the locals on their way to Swaffham market in the days before

the A47 (Norwich to King's Lynn) was built. Incidentally, most of these 'lost' sections of the original Peddars Way, including those in and around Merton and between Little Cressingham and North Pickenham, along with the present gaps at Palgrave, Castle Acre and Ringstead, have been missing for 200 years, if not more.

We know this because the sections were also missing when Mr Faden's men drew up his maps of 1797.

The A47 ends the daydreaming and thrusts one back into reality for you can hear it, or at least hear the incessant hum of passing traffic, before you actually see it. Once across, a surfaced lane leads by Grange Farm as far as Moat Farm, where the line disappears once again. While the walker has to detour around Bartholomew's Hills in order to reach Castle Acre, the old Way presumably reached the Nar crossing by taking some largely invisible line of descent from Hungry Hill which is, nevertheless, detectable on aerial photographs as cropmarks.

Castle Acre is a delightful stopping place, a village on a hill full of stone buildings and walls, a pretty green, an immaculately kept church, the romantic ruins of a Cluniac priory and a Norman motte and bailey castle, and some splendid pubs which have revived many an exhausted traveller over the years. However, it is best to avoid busy weekends in summer, for it is a very popular visitor attraction and parking can be difficult.

North of Castle Acre the actual line of the Way lies buried under the Massingham road (a debilitating three and a half mile uphill slog, though a headland path has been established as far as the Wicken), and not until Shepherd's Bush is reached does the traveller find safety and peace once again. Some of the best walking on the Way now stretches ahead for here, slowly and even hesitantly, the Peddars Way becomes a grassy, stoney track, sometimes wide, occasionally rutted, running between hedgerows, shelterbelts or cultivated fields.

It is hard if not impossible to suggest that this stretch represents the original width of the Roman road, or that here or there is a trace of the old agger, because over the centuries it has been regularly eroded, modified and repaired during the course of agricultural operations, and truth to tell it would be a surprise if anything of the original still existed. But it does still offer fine, subtle views and some cracking walking. The brilliant yellow of oilseed rape, the light blue of flax or linseed and the sepias of cereal crops, knuckles of flint and stones and scrapes of chalk, all help to give this portion of High Norfolk its atmosphere and colour. In the heat of summer the land sometimes looks squeezed dry of goodness, and irrigation gantries hover over the fields like giant insects. Along the field margins and among the many old marl pits, the endless tracks and lanes, hedgerows and woodlands offer refuges for wildlife, while overhead skylarks hover and sing in the big sky while rabbits patrol the margins of the fields.

Some of the trail's most satisfying walking is here as the Way leads one on with Roman certainty and purpose. The track is often wide and grassy and it seems to wallow in its own importance as a significant mark on the landscape. Mere villages and hamlets stand back in deference to it. It is also in these areas that the loss of the old wooden finger posts, or even the old concrete signposts, is noticed. Many of the circular logo discs - some of which were evidently used for airgun target practice - have gone, too, but at the time of writing new finger posts are being erected.

Over the A148 Fakenham road, past some brick and flint cottages, and then by Harpley Dams and Common, there are vast fields and, in spring, hedgerows snowy white with may blossom. The fields between Anmer Minque and the Houghton estate - delineated by a bold, wooded line to the east - are dotted with tumuli and swathed in greenery. Past Bircham, as the track finally closes in on Fring, the Way seems to puff itself up again and swell to even greater width. Then it gathers itself together and descends the slope in a series of uncharacteristic little dips and dives to the now miniscule remnant of the old Heacham river. Evidently susceptible to rainfall levels of earlier months - which explains why its state rarely seems to reflect current weather conditions - the little stream is either at full spate, which means it is a little over boot-top height, or it has retreated to become no more than a puddle. In fact there have been times when it has disappeared altogether.

This road junction is known as Fring Cross, but the Way ignores the village of Fring just as it ignores Sedgeford, and instead takes a dramatic, upward, curving line over the brow of the hill by Dovehill Wood, loses its way for a moment at Littleport, and then re-positions itself along the driveway beside Magazine House, a former 17th century magazine and powder store.

Ahead are more fields, more plantations, and for the walker, another minor diversion; and then a gentle desent into Ringstead, where another section is long lost. Sometimes, particularly in wet weather if the field is being ploughed, or if the crop and the light is right, you can stand near the row of houses where the road turns towards the old windmill, and look back towards the Docking road by Gedding's Farm and catch a fleeting glimpse of the former line of the old road as a cropmark or a faint pale line stretching across the furrows.

What is thought to be the original line of the Way is picked up yet again at the start of the signed diversion just beyond the mill which becomes a section of hedged track on what appears to be a slightly raised agger. Ahead lie views of the Wash and broad sweeps of the coastline, a sight which has helped banish exhaustion on a number of occasions. Then over the busy Hunstanton road and on to a metalled lane called Seagate, which marks the last discernible line of our Roman road before it finally reaches the sandy, buried mysteries of Holme beach and dunes.

The Way ahead

In attempting to measure just how far the Way has travelled in the last 2000 years it is necessary to refer to the early days and documents of the Peddars Way (and Coast Path), at the dawn of its career as a national trail leisure facility. In the only sort of dry tones allowed by consultation documents, Willie Wilson's 1980 summary stated merely that the proposals (for a national route) 'will provide a path of some 140 kilometres, of which approximately 43 kilometres will require the creation of new rights of way.' In a sense the management strategy document of 1996 was more confident but only marginally more forthcoming, quoting a Countryside Commission guideline that the purpose of national trails was to 'provide a nationally and

Right: Approaching its end. The Way reaches Holme beach

internationally recognised series of walks and rides through countryside of exceptional beauty, giving the highest quality of experience, and allowing both extended and shorter journeys within the same scenic corridor.'

This same strategy document did at least begin to grapple with the inevitable problems of information, education and promotion. Sites of particular interest ought to be mapped and interpretation (noticeboards, publications, etc) systems developed, it went on; perhaps there was also a need to establish if the route could be used as an educational tool (earth walks, art, drama); and then there was the difficulty of putting together a marketing package. Who was using the route? Who would use it? At whom should the advertising promotions be aimed?

A user survey carried out in 1995/96 attempted to find some of the answers. It refined the concept of the short distance user (SDU) and the long distance user (LDU) who, between them and during the survey period, evidently accounted for something like 103,000 user days on the trail. The categories were split roughly 87 per cent (short distance user) and 13 per cent (long). Of these, a considerable majority were walkers. Only seven per cent preferred cycling. As many as one in five chose to walk alone, about two-thirds were on holiday, and over a third lived more than 100 miles from the path. Nearly four per cent of the LDUs were overseas' visitors.

Of great significance, perhaps, the survey also underlined the fact that the largest age range category was between 45 and 59 years (over 35 per cent) with the 60-plusses (almost 30 per cent) second. Asked for their reasons for enjoying the route, the users nominated three attractions well above all the others. They came, they said, for the scenery and the landscape, for the nature (or natural history), and for plain and simple peace and quiet.

Still on the statistical front, the survey also suggested that the 80,000 users indicated during the survey period probably injected something like £1,500,000 into the local economy, the long distance walker category alone generating about £200,000. In addition, and taking the National Trail as a whole, 44 miles of the 93-mile route was available for horse riding, and 44 miles for cycling, while there was motorised access over 20 miles.

In the main the survey confirmed what I had sensed about the trail now that it was not new and had settled into respectability. Many of the young, 30-miles-a-day 'professional' yompers do not or have not used it because as a walking challenge it is classified as only 'moderate' in a sense that there are no peat bogs, wild moors or rock faces.

In other words, for some it is not extreme enough. On the other hand older categories have tended to choose it precisely for those very reasons. As a long distance walk it presents a relatively gentle and basically attainable challenge, with the added bonuses that it does have a quiet landscape, it boasts birds and the skyscapes, good pubs and (so I was once told by a group of newly retired, freshly-booted walkers from Leicester) some remarkably fine fish and chip shops. A second user survey being planned for 2002/03 may underline some of these things. But it is clear this is to be the immediate future of the old road, and I for one will not object. At least the road is still here.

You can learn a lot through the soles of your feet by walking your way into the heart of the past, and the fact that the Way is now being used for leisure while its past is beginning to inspire poets, artists, writers, musicians and photographers - as the book A Norfolk Songline suggests - is another indication that after 2000 years of ever-changing life it is in the process of reinventing itself yet again, adapting to a yet another new calling.

The evolution of this latest role as a leisure facility is a process which has been going on for two or three decades to the extent that it is now possible to say, after years of slumber, the old road has awakened again. Even in the 30 years since my first foray along its green and silent ways it has learned how to cope with mountain bikes and 'Romany' caravans, diversionary and concessionary paths, Campervans and lightweight tents, joggers and Venture Scouts, charity walkers and school parties, fitness freaks and dog walkers, camp sites and boardwalks, RUPPs (roads used as public path), mobile phones and litter, waymarks and Gortex clothing, marketing strategies and user surveys, strollers and horses, picnics and metal detectors, stiles and crisp packets; and, some years ago, with at least one perplexed and perspiring Dutchman on a bicycle who, having diverted from his planned holiday excursion route to King's Lynn, had toiled along a bumpy section of the Peddars Way in North West Norfolk in search of a castle. 'What castle?' we asked.

'I don't know,' he said, 'but a signpost pointing along this track said Ancient Monument.'

He had ridden 10 miles in his determination to find it. Perseverance, that's the thing. Perseverance, and peace and quiet.

Journey over, and the end of the road. The Peddars Way peters out at Holme Dunes at the edge of the sea

Reading and References

I have labelled this a Reading and Reference list rather than a Bibliography because from the point of view of subject it offers a range of things from a sweep of general background to local detail and on to passing reference. Thus the relevance of the titles includes everything from a complete book or essay down in some cases to a single sentence. Nevertheless, within this list the reader will find much about Seahenge, Boudica, the Iron Age and Roman Norfolk, Roman roads in general and the Peddars Way in particular. Take your pick.

Ashwin, Trevor. Excavations at Scole (article). The Quarterly. Norfolk Archaeological & Historical Research Group, No 26, 1997

Barrett, David (article). Eastern Daily Press Seahenge pull-out. January 14, 1999

Barringer, JC. Bryant's Map of Norfolk in 1826. The Larks Press, 1998

Barringer, JC. Faden's Map of Norfolk, 1797. The Larks Press, 1989

Berresford Ellis, John. The Druids. Constable, 1994

Bonser, KJ. The Drovers. County Book Club, 1972

Bridges, EM. Norfolk Norfolk Coast. The Geographical Association, 1998

Brennard, Mark & Taylor, Maisie (article, Seahenge). Current Archaeology, No 167, 2000

Brown, Robin. Field Walking at Woodcock Hall (article). Norfolk Archaeological Rescue Group News, No 10, 1977

Brown, Robin. The Claudian Fort at Woodcock Hall (article). The Quarterly, No 20, Norfolk Archaeological & Historical Research Group, 1995

Brown, Robin. Saham Saga (Saham Toney newsletter; article). October, 1996

Brown, Robin. Shadows on the Grass (extract, from A History of Saham Toney). Limited publication, 1998

Chadburn, Amanda. The Iceni and their Coins (article). The Quarterly, No 17, Norfolk Archaeological & Historical Research Group, 1995

Chadburn, Amanda & Gurney, David. The Fring Coin Hoard (article). Norfolk Archaeology, vol 61, part 2, 1991

Champion, Matthew. Seahenge: A Contemporary Chronicle. Barnwell's Timescape, 2000

Chevallier, Raymond. Roman Roads. Batsford, 1989

Clarke, RR. In Breckland Wilds. 2nd edition. EP Publishing, 1974

Clarke, WG. Peddars Way (article). Proceedings, vol 2, part 1, Prehistoric Society of East Anglia, 1915

Clover, RD. Dim Corridors. Geo R Reeve, 1948

Clover, RD. Peddars Way. Eastern Daily Press, April 30, 1947; Wayside Story. Eastern Daily Press, July 11, 1981

Coles, John & Hall, David. Changing Landscapes: The Ancient Fenland. Cambridgeshire County Council, 1998

Cook, Olive. Breckland. Hale, 1980

Countryside Commission. The Peddars Way & Norfolk Coast Path: a consultation paper, 1980

Countryside Commission & Norfolk County Council. Peddars Way & Norfolk Coast Path national trail user survey summary of results, 1996

Curl, Joan (article). Along the Peddars Way. Country Life, November 30, 1951

Current Archaeology. No 151, Scaftworth article, 1997; No 169, Kennewick article, 2000

Dark, Ken & Dark, Petra. The Landscape of Roman Britain. Sutton Publishing, 1998

Davies, John. Iron Age Norfolk (article). The Quarterly, No 15, Norfolk Archaeological & Historical Research Group, 1994

Davies, John. History of Coins Reveals Secrets. Eastern Daily Press, October 18, 1997

Davies, John & Williamson, Tom. Land of the Iceni: The Iron Age in Northern East Anglia. Centre of East Anglian Studies, 1999

Davison, Alan. Norfolk Origins 5: Deserted Villages in Norfolk. Poppyland, 1996

de Bootman, Michael. Re-evaluation of Romano-British Villa at Gayton Thorpe, Norfolk (article). Norfolk Archaeology, vol 62, part 4, 1998

Dymond, David. The Norfolk Landscape. Hodder & Stoughton, 1985

Eastern Daily Press (story). Court Decision on Peddars Way. March 28, 1951

Eastern Evening News (article). Journey of Discovery down Peddars Way. October 23, 1946

Edwards, DA & Wade Martins, Peter. Norfolk From the Air. Norfolk Museums Service, 1987

Edwards, Derek & Wade Martins, Peter. Norfolk From the Air, vol 2. Norfolk Museums Service, 1999

Fiske, RC. The Enclosure at Ashill (article). NARG News, No 29, Norfolk Archaeological Rescue Group, 1982

Flitcroft, Mik. The Roman Small Towns of Norfolk (article).The Quarterly, No 23, Norfolk Archaeological & Historical Research Group, 1996

Forrest, AJ. Under Three Crowns. Boydell, 1961

Fraser, Antonia. Boadicea's Chariot. Weidenfeld & Nicholson, 1988

Frere, Sheppard. Britannia. Pimlico, 1991

Grant, Sally. Boudicca. The Larks Press, 1995

Gregory, Tony. Romano-British Settlement in West Norfolk and the Norfolk Fen Edge (monograph). BAR British Series, No 103, 1982

Gregory, Tony. An enclosure of the 1st century AD at Thornham. East Anglian Archaeology. EAA 30, Norfolk Museums Service, 1986

Gregory, Tony. The Enclosure at Ashill (article). East Anglian Archaeology, No 5, 1977

Haines, Carol. Marking the Miles: A History of English Milestones. Carol Haines, 2000

Hammond, Jane & Barnett, Steve (article). From Fring to Heacham. The Annual, No 5, Norfolk Archaeological & Historical Research Group, 1996

Hannigan, Des. Ancient Tracks. Tiger Books, 1994

Hooton, Jonathan. The Glaven Ports. Blakeney History Group, 1996

Ireland, S. Roman Britain, a Sourcebook (2nd edition). Routledge, 1996

Keys, David (article). The Independent, June 28, 2000

Keys, David (article). The Independent on Sunday, November 5, 2000

Keys, David (article). Revealed: the Earliest London of them All. The Independent on Sunday, December 24, 2000

Keys, David (article). Archaeologists hunt for Roman troop ship. The Independent, April 19, 2001

Kightly, Charles. Folk Heroes of Britain. Thames & Hudson, 1982

King, John. Kingdoms of the Celts. Blandford, 2000

Lawson, Andrew J (introduction). Prehistoric Earthworks in Norfolk. Prehistoric Society, 1978

Lewton-Brain, CH. A Mixed Bag (article). Eastern Daily Press, December 20, 1975

Livingstone, Helen. In the Footsteps of Caesar: Walking Roman Roads in Britain. Dial House, 1995

Lupton, Hugh & McGowan, Liz. A Norfolk Songline: Walking the Peddars Way. Hickathrift Books, 1999

Mardle, Jonathan (Eric Fowler) (articles). The Peddars Way 1 & 2. Eastern Daily Press, September 9 & September 16, 1959

Margary, Ivan D. Roman Roads in Britain. Baker, 1973

Margeson, Sue & Ayers, Brian & Heywood, Stephen (editors). A Festival of Norfolk Archaeology. Norfolk & Norwich Archaeological Society, 1996

Margeson, Sue & Seillier, Fabienne & Rogerson, Andrew. The Normans and Norfolk. Norfolk Museums Service, 1994

Mason HJ & McClelland, A. A Background to Breckland. Providence Press, 1994

Moore, Ivan. The Archaeology of Suffolk. Suffolk County Council, 1988

Morton, HV. In Search of England. Methuen, 1927

Norfolk County Council. Peddars Way & Norfolk Coast Path management strategy. 1996

Norfolk County Council. Access to Peddars Way & Norfolk Coast Path by public transport. 1994

Ordnance Survey Historical Map & Guide, Roman Britain. Ordnance Survey, 1991

Patterson, Frank (illustrations). Britain's Counties: Norfolk. GM Design, 1993

Peel, JHB. Along the Roman Roads of Britain. Pan, 1971

Peddars Way & Norfolk Coast Path User Survey (summary). Norfolk County Council, 1996

Peddie, John. Invasion. Guild Publishing, 1987

Peddie, John. The Roman War Machine. Alan Sutton Publishing, 1994

Pollitt, Michael (article). Eastern Daily Press, August 6, 1996

Pryor, Francis. Seahenge. HarperCollins, 2001

Rainbird Clarke, R. In Breckland Wilds. 2nd edition, EP Publishing, 1974

Robinson, Bruce. Chasing the Shadows: Norfolk Mysteries Revisited. Elmstead Publications, 1996

Robinson, Bruce. The Alignment of Norfolk's Peddars Way in Relation to Natural Watercourses (short paper, unpublished), 1997

Robinson, Bruce. The Peddars Way. Weathercock Press, 1978

Robinson, Bruce. The Peddars Way & Norfolk Coast Path. Aurum Press, 1992

Robinson, Bruce. The Norfolk Walker's Book. Elmstead Publications, 1998

Robinson, Bruce & Gregory, Tony. Celtic Fire & Roman Rule. Poppyland, 1987

Robinson, Bruce & Rose, Edwin. Roads & Tracks. Poppyland, 1983

Salway, Peter. The Oxford Illustrated History of Roman Britain. BCA, 1993

Sauer, Eberhard. Alchester (article). Current Archaeology, No 173, April, 2001

Scarfe, Norman. The Suffolk Landscape. Hodder & Stoughton, 1975

Sealey, Paul. The Boudican Revolt Against Rome. Shire Archaeology, 1997

Selkirk, Raymond. On the Trail of the Legions. Anglia

Publishing, 1995

Sim, Judy. Rebellion Against Rome (article). The Quarterly, No 19, Norfolk Archaeological & Historical Research Group, 1995

Skipper, Kate & Williamson, Tom. Thetford Forest. Centre of East Anglian Studies, 1997

Smallwood, John. De Civitate Icenorum (article). NARG News, No 20, Norfolk Archaeological Rescue Group, 1980

Smallwood, John. Roman Settlements in North West Norfolk (article). NARG News, No 25, Norfolk Archaeological Rescue Group, 1981

Somerset Fry, Plantagenet. Boudicca. Allen, 1978

Somerset Fry, Plantagenet. Rebellion Against Rome. Dalton, 1982

Spence, Lewis. Boadicea: Warrior Queen of the Britons. Hale, 1937

Tacitus. The Annals of Imperial Rome. Penguin Classics, 1989

Tacitus. Tacitus on Britain and Germany. Penguin Classics, 1948

Wacher, John. Roman Britain. Dent, 1980

Wacher, John. The Towns of Roman Britain. Book Club Associates, 1976

Wade-Martins, Peter (editor). An Historical Atlas of Norfolk. Norfolk Museums Service, 1993

Wade-Martins, Peter. Norfolk Century (article). Easter Daily Press, 1999

Wade-Martins, Peter. The Linear Earthworks of West Norfolk. Reprint from Norfolk Archaeology, vol 34, part 1, 1974

Wade-Martins, Susanna. A History of Norfolk. Phillimore, 1984

Wade-Martins, Susanna. A Mardle about Marl Pits (article). Eastern Daily Press, March 9, 1996

Webster, Graham. Boudica. Batsford, 1978

Webster, Graham. The Roman Imperial Army. University of Oklahoma, 1998

West, John. Roman Lincoln. Watkins, 1991

Whatmore, Rev Leonard E. Highway to Walsingham. The Pilgrim Bureau, 1973

Williamson, Tom. The Origins of Norfolk. Manchester University Press, 1993

Williamson, Tom & Smallwood, John (articles). The Annual, No 6, Norfolk Archaeological & Historical Research Group, 1997

Wilkens, Imam. Where Troy Once Stood. Rider, 1990

Woodward, Ann. Shrines & Sacrifice. English Heritage, 1992

Yaxley, David (editor). Survey of the Houghton Hall Estate, by Joseph Hill, 1800. Norfolk Record Society, volume L, 1984

Information

The 150km Peddars Way and Norfolk Coast Path national trail is supported by The Countryside Agency and Norfolk and Suffolk County Councils. Locally, under the auspices of Norfolk County Council's planning and transportation department, it is administered from:

The National Trail Office
6 Station Road
Wells next the Sea
Norfolk
NR23 1AE
Tel: 01328 711533
Fax: 01328 710182
E-mail: peddars.way@dial.pipex.com
Website: www.countryside.gov.uk
National Trail manager: Tim Lidstone-Scott
National Trail assistant: Patrick J Saunders

A number of helpful publications and leaflets relating to the Peddars Way and the National Trail are available from the above address. These include:

National Trails: An introduction to National Trail routes in England and Wales (booklet). The Countryside Agency

The Peddars Way and Norfolk Coast Path (brochure). The Countryside Agency

A Norfolk Songline: Walking the Peddars Way (stories, poetry, photographs; book and CD). See: Reading & References

Peddars Way and Norfolk Coast Path management strategy (report). Norfolk County Council

Peddars Way and Norfolk Coast Path users survey 1996 (report). Norfolk County Council

Peddars Way & Norfolk Coast Path marketing strategy 1999 (report). The Countryside Agency, Norfolk & Suffolk County Councils

Volunteer Ranger Scheme (explanatory leaflet). The National Trail Office

Walk Free (leaflet; a service to walkers). Walkfree, Swaffham

The Peddars Way and Norfolk Coast Path official guide for walkers, published by Aurum Press, is also listed among Reading & References. Details about the accommodation guide, circular walks, disabled access and public transport guides may be obtained from The National Trail Office.